LONDON TRANSPORT

BUSES & COACHES

1960

LONDON TRANSPORT

BUSES & COACHES

1960

Includes supplement to some
earlier books in the series

John A.S. Hambley

Published in 2001 by
JOHN A.S. HAMBLEY
7 Linden Road,
Dunstable,
Beds. LU5 4NZ

© JOHN HAMBLEY

Additional text and research by David A. Ruddom

British Library Cataloguing in Publication Data
A catalogue record for this book is available from the British Library

ISBN 095331465 0

Designed and produced by Hedgehog.
Printed and bound in Great Britain.

Two RTs with RT3 type bodywork purr their way along Woburn Place on their respective routes with the lead bus journeying to South Croydon, Earl of Eldon. Except for a slightly different colour scheme and out of use number plate holder on the corner of the front nearside bulkhead, RT343 looks very much as it did when first entering service in March 1948. The Park Royal body, numbered 1572, initially carried by sister vehicle RT323, would stay married to the chassis for the final few years service in the capital and its eventual export in 1964. (Photobus)

With GR303 running plates, RF271 continues its journey through Watford High Street on Route 719 sometime during the brief period it was garaged at Garston between May and August of the year now under review. Outshopped from overhaul in May this picture raises an interesting question. In August it was one of the sixteen coaches painted in an experimental livery of two shades of lighter green which appeared from Reigate and High Wycombe on Route 711. It is difficult to tell from a black and white photograph but was the coach repainted again in August or is it running here in its new livery on the 719, pre-empting the main experiment? It is also interesting that the chassis and body here is that of the original RF113. At its next visit to Aldenham the chassis and body would be parted the former going to RF96 and the latter to RF278. Which just proves that with RTs and RFs you never quite knew what you were looking at! (A.Mortimer)

Acknowledgements

This particular volume brings a certain amount of satisfaction in as much as it fills the gap in this series of books which follows the history of London Transport bus and coach operations from 1939 through to 1962. In no small way the series benefited from the expert knowledge of many historians and photographers, to all of whom I extend a wholehearted thank you. My very good friend David Ruddom whose tireless efforts translate into the very readable captions must be singled out as the spur to motivate me to continue the series and I must thank him for all the very hard work he has contributed. The following photographic sources have been used to compile this survey of bus and coach operation in 1960. I should therefore like to pay due acknowledgement to: James H.Aston, the late G.E.Baddeley, Dave Berwick, 'Bespix', Alan B.Cross, A.J.Douglas, Michael Dryhurst, J.Firth, R.A.Golds, Roy Hobbs, Roger Holmes, John Gascoine, John C.Gillham, Fred W.Ivey, D.A.Jones, Kevin Lane, the late Bill Legg, John Lines, L.T.P.S., LCC Tramways Trust, the late R.F.Mack, P.J.Malsher, C.S.Marshall, Alan Mortimer, S.A.Newman, Omnibus Society, Tony R.Packer, Pamlin Prints, Douglas F.Parker, K.V.Partridge, B.Pask, I.Pearce, T.Peart, 'Photobus', 'Photomatic', Norman Rayfield, Michael Rooum, D.A.Ruddom., R.H.G.Simpson, Surfleet Transport Photographs, Michael A.Sutcliffe the late D.A.Thompson and Ron Wellings. Factual information has been gleaned from many published sources of information and it follows that in particular I would wish to thank and gratefully acknowledge the London Historical Research Group of the Omnibus Society, the London Omnibus Traction Society, the PSV Circle, Peter Gomm of the RT/RF Register and the Transport Interests Publishers. On a more personal note, a warm hearted thank you to my wife Iris and David Ruddom's wife Enid for all the patience they show to two rather obsessed transport historians.

Publishers Note

It is gratifying to record that still more photographers have come forward with further unpublished material suitable for use in this series of books. If you do have unpublished prints or negatives, be it a solitary item or many, which you feel would be interesting to other enthusiasts, then please do forward them to me at the address shown at the beginning of this book. Kevin Lane has been involved with the printing of many of the pictures used throughout this series of books and can be relied upon for all your black and white photographic services.

Introduction

The trolleybus replacement programme continued throughout the year providing the main emphasis to the changing scene of bus operation within the Central Area of London Transport. A total of 439 RMs were delivered to the Executive and used to replace trolleybuses whose numbers were depleted with the further disposal of 419 vehicles. Not to be outshone, the Country Area introduced a number of experimental concepts. Three experimental dual doored AEC Reliances with Willowbrook 42 seat bodies entered service at Two Waters garage in September. These were given the class letters RW and segregated boarding and alighting passengers resulting in greatly improved 'dwell time' at bus stops. This was a problem that had been experienced with the six years of operation by the converted single door OMO RFs. Nearly a year after they had been repainted into green livery, the batch of RTLs finally entered service in July marking the first regular use of the class in the Country Area. They provided the bulk of the double deck requirement of Hatfield garage. Sixteen Green Line RFs together with CRL4 received an experimental livery of two lighter shades of green during the year as part of an evaluation of new types of paint which had been developed by the manufacturers. To provide additional double deck buses for relief duties a total of twenty-eight RTs were repainted into Green Line livery during the year similar to the long standing examples in East London but with simple transfers rather than the raised metal motif carried between decks.

The fitting of flashing trafficators to the bus and coach fleet was completed during the year, the only exceptions being the then current training fleet and those vehicles earmarked for early withdrawal. Concurrently the move towards universally painted garage codes in place of stencil plates on Central Area vehicles gathered momentum although it would be a few years yet before the Country Area adopted the idea. A further innovation adopted in 1960 was the introduction of bright orange plastic slip boards reading 'Pay As You Enter' which began to replace the previously almost unreadable transfers fixed to window areas near the front of vehicles.

The great majority of Central Area route changes were linked to the continuing replacement of trolleybuses by diesel engined buses and four further stages took place during the year. One other change reflected both the burgeoning development of the road infrastructure in London alongside the increasing congestion. This was the shortening in October of the Blackwall Tunnel 108 route and the introduction of a 108B solely operating on the south side of the river to avoid the excessive delays of the tunnel which at this stage was still a single two-way bore. At the same time the new fly-under and approach road to the north of the tunnel was constructed, the works resulting in more delays. Throughout the whole of London Transport deteriorating staff levels and recruitment problems played a part in some service cutbacks. October 1960 saw the night routes which were numbered in the 280 and 290 series losing their 200 numbers in favour of an 'N' prefix so that 290 became N90 and so on. This released a further twenty numbers for use in the ongoing trolleybus replacement programme.

Two very different groups of vehicles were rehoused during the year. The BEA fleet of AEC Regal IV half deck coaches operated under contract by London Transport was moved from Shepherds Bush garage to the now defunct Hammersmith trolleybus depot which was converted for the purpose. At the other extreme the preserved fleet of vehicles stored for many years at Reigate garage was moved to the former Clapham garage, which had closed in 1958, in readiness for the new British Transport Commission's Museum of Transport which would open on the site.

By the end of the year the bus and coach fleet composition had changed with the disposal of 55 RTs of the 2RT2 variety, a solitary RTL following fire damage, 24 TDs and 5 Ts balanced by the previously referred to new deliveries. The single deckers were destined for export and further service in Ceylon. These figures clearly demonstrate that standardisation of the entire road passenger carrying fleet was now in sight and that in around two years time the fleet would consist of just seven basic types of bus and coach.

With the driver poised to release the handbrake, RTL641 is about to depart Shepherds Bush Road en-route to Sandown Park as a Race Special from Shepherds Bush Green on a Saturday in June. After a final overhaul in April 1962 and its twilight years spent operating out of Bow garage, the bus would be disposed of in October 1965, having completed fifteen years plus serving the capital. (M.Dryhurst)

After a very short period of a couple of months in passenger service operating from Tottenham garage on Route 76 with possible occasional forays on to the 34B, RM44 was re-assigned to learner duties until October 1962. It alternated between Upton Park and West Ham until it re-entered passenger service on a permanent basis as a trolleybus replacement, its original intended purpose. Seen here in November during a spell spent at West Ham, it has turned out of Chiswick High Road into the Gunnersbury roundabout beneath trolleybus wiring for the 655, 657 and 667 routes. (M.Dryhurst)

Stage five of the trolleybus conversion programme took place early in February affecting West Ham and Walthamstow depots. Seen on what until a few days previous had been the Routes 689/690 stand at Stratford, West Ham garaged RM6 waits departure for East Ham, White Horse on Route 272. This route replaced half of the erstwhile circular trolleybus routes and continued beyond the White Horse during Monday to Friday rush hours to the Royal Albert Dock, enhancing services already provided by Routes 101 and 147. Originally delivered to Aldenham Works in June 1959 the bus still serves the capital to this day, now in the colours of Arriva London. (M.Dryhurst)

Route 234A had been operated by the RF class of bus since the single deck LT class buses were removed in January 1953, thus ending the last official allocation of the type for passenger service within the capital. RF412, one of the original allocation to Croydon garage for the conversion of the route, will soon have completed a further journey over its familiar roads as it heads across the junction at Purley Fountain on 19th November bound for Old Lodge Lane. (A.R.Packer)

Looking as good as new, having received an overhaul during March, RT644 re-entered service at Two Waters having spent its earlier years garaged at Grays and then Amersham. Not surprisingly, this Sunday duty looks as if it is likely to complete its journey to Watford Heath without passengers, having only a short distance further to run from this Watford town centre bus stop. (A.Mortimer)

The original open air market together with the still uncompleted 'Great Harry' public house, provide an interesting background to RT3892 as it rests in the Hemel Hempstead bus station on 15th October. It is working one of the through journeys on the 318 via the villages west of the A41 to Watford and then north again to Abbots Langley. This bus was allocated to Garston for almost ten years but would later be outshopped from overhaul in the red livery of the Central Area. (A.R.Packer)

The Daimler chassis of former D156 now carries a 1956 Harkness built body in place of the Duple example fitted when it first entered service in March 1946. One hundred of the D class were acquired by Belfast Corporation, all of which were rebodied giving many years of extended service in their adopted homeland. This city centre scene, with the prominent YMCA building to the left of the picture, depicts the bus journeying to Crumlin Road, a location synonymous with the civil unrest of more recent years. (D.F.Parker)

Night route 286 had been introduced in the tram replacement programme of 7th October 1951. The service operated between Charing Cross L.T. Station and New Cross via Camberwell with three journeys extended to Brockley Rise. Peckham garage used three RTs to cover the operation and RT370 is seen on Victoria Embankment near the station on 2nd July en-route for the more usual destination. (A.R.Packer)

The 1960 style retail activity in Watford provides the background to RT3867 which looks well laden for its journey to Oxhey Estate on Route 346A. This picture is a fine example of the standard appearance of the RT fleet in 1960 throughout London, whether green or red. The Country Area vehicles were distinguishable by their green mudguards as against the black of the Central Area and their green radiator triangle badges. (A.Mortimer)

Hanwell garage (HL), the former trolleybus depot, had initially opened as a tram shed but since November of the year under review the occupants have been RM buses for use on Routes 207, 207A and 255. RM478 is seen under the now defunct trolleybus wiring on the Uxbridge Road near Southall as it journeys to Shepherds Bush Green along the route of the former electric service 607. (A.R.Packer)

RT759 had received its final overhaul in July 1959 to re-enter service at New Cross garage where it was to complete its years of service with London Transport. It then remained in the capital from September 1964 being used by Seth Coaches of Kentish Town. At New Cross Gate it waits for a new crew before continuing its journey to Plumstead Common on Route 53. RT3329, having drawn up behind, will continue its journey to Abbey Wood on Route 177. One wonders whether the Roma Grill bears any resemblance to similar establishments in the more exotic location of the Italian capital whose name it bears. (A.Mortimer)

RLH49 heads across the railway bridge at Maryland Point commencing a journey to Clapton Pond on Route 178. By the time this late summer view was taken the trolleybus wiring had been removed. Between overhauls this RLH received a repaint from green to red livery along with three others made surplus to Country Area requirements since the strike of 1958. They entered service at Dalston garage along with several others of the class already wearing the appropriate livery on this route when it was introduced in place of the 208A on 13th May 1959. (J.A.S.Hambley collection)

Passengers board West Green garaged RTL96 at Victoria Station on Saturday 25th June for a journey on Route 29. The bus is working to Cockfosters, the most northerly point reached direct from Victoria weekdays when the route was operated in two sections. Buses to South Mimms and Borehamwood usually started at Turnpike Lane Station. The RTL shown here would receive a further overhaul in October 1964, eventually being dispatched to the Wombwell Diesel Company for scrap in June 1969. (A.R.Packer)

In an attempt to alleviate the effects of congestion in the Blackwall Tunnel, new services on sections of route south of the tunnel which would not be involved in the passage under the Thames were introduced with the winter programme on 12th October. The long standing 228 between Chislehurst and Eltham was extended to Surrey Docks on Monday to Friday and a 228A variant introduced terminating at the south entrance to Blackwall Tunnel. Recently overhauled RT1111, now garaged at Sidcup, is seen working a duty on new Route 228A but its via point blind is that of the old shorter 228 route. (R.Wellings)

The six STLs acquired by Grimsby Corporation in August 1955 were the last double deck buses to be purchased before the Grimsby-Cleethorpes Joint Transport Committee came into being on 1st January 1957. Coats of arms of both towns are carried on the lower panels and former STL2695, now fourteen year old, still looks very spruce as it waits at the traffic lights in Riby Square, Grimsby. (Mike A.Sutcliffe)

The red liveried 41 seat Central Area bus versions of the RF entered passenger service in late 1952 and early 1953 and were numbered from RF289 to RF513. In March 1956 RF289 to 294 were converted to Green Line coaches with the addition of saloon doors, luggage racks, brackets for route side boards and had their seating reduced to forty. An already well laden RF293 in its Green Line livery takes on more passengers at Purley before continuing its journey to East Grinstead on Route 708. (A.R.Packer)

About to continue its journey on Route 321 working to Maple Cross, RT3449 pauses in Watford. The via blind has been untidily set between two of the displays intended for the route which continues to provide the trunk service between Luton and Watford. At the time of writing it is largely worked by environmentally friendly LPG powered DAF single deck vehicles with prominent roof mounted tanks. (A.Mortimer)

Having initially entered service in June 1950, RLH12 would spend its entire passenger carrying years officially garaged at Addlestone together with eight months in disuse awaiting disposal which took place in February 1966. On loan to Guildford garage it stands in Onslow Street Bus Station working one of the additional journeys which were introduced to Route 436 on 20th July of the year under review between Guildford and Burpham, turning there via New Inn Lane, Glendale Drive and Winterhill Way. (J.A.S.Hambley collection)

RT4092 stands abandoned in Green Lanes just south of Manor House, which suggests that a relief crew was not expected to be available and so the previous team only worked the bus to this point from Bruce Grove. The 171 route originated as a replacement for one of the Kingsway Subway tram services and Holloway Depot always had a small allocation on these routes which the buses continued despite the fact that the 171 did not run very close to Holloway. The tradition of a Holloway allocation carried on until November 1961 when the six North London duties on the route were more logically moved to West Green and Tottenham. (F.W.Ivey)

Route 278 had been introduced with stage six of the trolleybus conversion programme towards the end of April with RM buses garaged at West Ham although on this occasion an RT is being used. RT1785 was one of the buses gained by West Ham when Forest Gate garage closed in April and it is seen here at Connaught Road Victoria and Albert Docks terminus on 23rd October. (A.R.Packer)

This interesting scene at Kingsbury Square, Aylesbury shows three familiar buses, two of which are operating for their second owner. From left to right, Country Area RT610 departs on its journey to Watford Junction by way of trunk route 301. It is about to pass ex-RT231 and it's battered roof companion ex-RT1519 in service with Red Rover. Both of the sold vehicles lack trafficators as fitted to RT610 while the Craven bodied example nearest the camera has lost its roof box. (F.W.Ivey)

Two RTs on Route 341 stand in Hatfield Station forecourt on Saturday 27th August. RT1090 on the left bound for the ultimate destination at St. Albans of Marshalswick while RT624 on the right will only work to the garage. This latter RT is an interloper on the route being from St. Albans garage and is one of the additional late Saturday afternoon journeys which were worked by SA off the 330 allocation. The 341 route was usually the responsibility of Hatfield and Hertford. Later in their lives both buses operated in red livery. RT1090 eventually went for scrap while 624 had the honour of being the very last RT on the last scheduled route, 62 from Barking and continued its life into preservation. (A.R.Packer)

A warm Wednesday evening in June sees RM224 at the Manor House terminal of new route 123 formerly used by trolleybus 623. A U-turn across Seven Sisters Road will be made to reach the departure stop, a manoeuvre which would be inconceivable today at this point. The bus is classified 4/5RM5/4, of which 150 were built, transmission, alternator and control panel being of CAV Ltd. manufacture, while the brake system was supplied by Lockheed. (M.Dryhurst)

Route 162 was introduced on 3rd February with the fifth stage of the trolleybus replacement programme. It replaced half of the 689/690 circular route, running via Plashet Road and Green Street to East Ham and then continuing to Barking after which it replaced the leg of Route 62 which ran to Little Heath. 162 was therefore a convenient number to use, at least for that end of the route. West Ham garage provided a daily allocation of new Routemasters which were supplemented on Monday to Friday by four RTs from Barking, which were in effect refugees from the former 62 allocation. In the upper picture RM26 waits on the traditional stand at Stratford Broadway used by the former trolleybuses and the trams before them. With the next conversion on 27th April extra stand space was needed and so the 162 and 272 routes found a new resting place in Tramway Avenue. It is on this stand that Barking's RT3791 is seen below. (J.A.S.Hambley collection and A.R.Packer)

Use of the islands originally erected for tram passengers at Turnpike Lane Station still provided a handy connection between bus and tube. RTL1590 delivered to London Transport in September 1954 eventually entered service at Upton Park garage in March 1958 and was transferred to its present home of West Green twelve months later. This June view shows it about to depart with a few passengers on Route 217 to Alexandra Park (Victoria) complete with wheel trims which have managed to avoid the painter's red oxide paint. Note the low placed bus stop signs all empty of individual route plates, possibly collected by a saver of such memorabilia or removed by local vandals.

(M.Dryhurst)

RTL1060 on the night route 290 stops in front of the imposing structure of the National Gallery en-route for its home base on 2nd July. Most of its operational career would be spent at Tottenham garage with only approximately two and a half years residence at Chalk Farm or West Green garage before withdrawal in December 1962. This RTL originally entered service with London Transport as RTL1059 and despite its change of number was one of many marriages of chassis and body which stayed together throughout their existence. (A.R.Packer)

RT4224 is seen on the opposite side of the road at Uxbridge in the same wet conditions as RF536 seen elsewhere in this volume. It waits departure for West Drayton Station on this Sunday service of Route 223. The lack of potential passengers is indicative of the reduction in Sunday services prevalent at the time. (A.Mortimer)

The transfer to Muswell Hill garage in January of a substantial number of RTs for the conversion of Route 212 from single to double deck operation included no fewer than seven which were returning from temporary loan to the Country Area. RT1269, seen at Wells Terrace, Finsbury Park during December, was one of these, having been previously at Addlestone, and its stay at MH would last until June 1963. The advertisement hoarding, partly obscured by the bus, refers to the lost pastime of ballroom dancing which was available in 'London's newest and gayest ballroom' - hardly a phrase that would be used nowadays. (A.R.Packer)

The practice of putting advertisements above the windows on RFs may have increased revenue but greatly spoilt their appearance. RF536, so treated, stands at the almost deserted Uxbridge terminal of Route 222. Originally entering service as a Country Area bus in April 1953 it had been transferred to the central Area and repainted in 1958 along with five of its contemporaries. The one pedestrian, casually strolling behind the bus has obviously spotted the photographer taking the low angled picture. (A.Mortimer)

Beginning in August of the year currently under review through to the following April, several AEC RT type buses spent varying lengths of time at the normally all Leyland Walworth garage while many RTLs were away being overhauled. RT4465 re-entered service in August after a planned visit to Aldenham, having previously been allocated to Sutton garage. It was to depart from Walworth the following March to join others of its class, firstly at Abbey Wood, then Alperton but not before it was captured on film at Victoria on 24th September blinded for a slightly shortened working on Route 185 to Greenwich Church. (W.R.Legg)

The oddly named company of Brown's Blue based at Markfield acquired a small number of the earliest post-war RTs with Weymann or Park Royal bodywork which appeared on the secondhand market in 1958. Former RT420 with added platform doors stands in their yard with ex-RT410 parked in the distance. All its previous owner's identity had been removed and a sticker on the bulkhead window indicates its use as a school bus, a far cry from its earlier arduous duties in the capital. (S.A.Newman)

Trolleybus wiring presents a surrealistic arch over Alperton's RT1935 as it negotiates the road system at the Jubilee Clock, Harlesden while continuing on its Route 18 journey to Edgware Station. The rather narrow Harlesden High Street is still two-way in 1960 and while the buildings may have looked elegant if not classical when new, the hotchpotch of shops and pedestrian barriers spoils the original designer's concept. The slipboard on the bus reads 'To and from Wembley Pool and Stadium' which, while served as the weekday terminal, was rather avoided by the Sunday route from London Bridge which is being worked here. (R.Wellings)

Well laden RFW13 is seen on private hire duty carrying a roundel sticker overprinted with 'SS 22'. The informative temporary road sign points to a fish market but which one and where has so far eluded the compilers of this book. Perhaps some reader can identify the town for us. Initially entering service in June 1951 and receiving overhauls in January 1956 and April 1961, this RFW had its operation with London Transport cut short in December 1964 when it was disposed of for further use in Ceylon. (R.F.Mack)

RT2088 is working the Sunday version of Route 95 numbered 95A, which was introduced in November 1958 to provide a service from south London to the Sunday markets around Petticoat Lane. This view of Aldgate High Street was taken on Boxing Day which accounts for the distinct lack of activity at this normally busy point. The bus itself achieved a commendable twenty-one year's service before Wombwell Diesels reduced it to scrap. (A.R.Packer)

The general appearance of RT642 indicates that some years have elapsed since it last received attention at the hands of the workforce of Aldenham Works. It is seen outside its home garage in St. Albans laying over between journeys on Route 313 to Enfield. In a few weeks time it will be despatched for its much needed overhaul and will return for its final spell of London Transport duty allocated to Luton. (A.Mortimer)

While resting at West Croydon Station on 17th April, RT457 demonstrates a different approach to the carrying of the duty number plate. The particular siting of the offside route number plate holder reveals that the original Weymann bodywork is now replaced by one of Saunders' manufacture but the roof box retains something of the vehicle's initial 1948 appearance. After two further overhauls the bus was finally scrapped by the workforce of Wombwell Diesels in January 1972. (Pamlin Prints)

Country Area RF674 first entered service in October 1953 at East Grinstead garage as a 41 seat bus. During June 1958 seating was reduced to 39 with the conversion to one man operation and the presently unused brackets for carrying the 'Pay as you board' sign can be seen below the nearside front windscreen. On a bright October day in the year under review it is seen on temporary loan to the Central Area with two-man crew in use on Route 218, having just left Kingston Bus Station at the start of its journey to Staines via Laleham. Other road users from left to right are a Wolseley 1500, an Austin A40 Somerset and an RT en-route to Chessington Zoo by way of Route 65. (A.Mortimer)

Three AEC Reliances with Willowbrook bodies given fleet numbers RW1 to 3 were obtained in 1960 and used on a variety of routes to test the suitability of one person operation in conjunction with a dual-door layout. The trio initially entered service in September of the year under review at Two Waters garage alongside conventional one man operated RFs on the 322 and 322A routes. RW2 is seen at the end of its journey in Hemel Hempstead Bus Station sometime during October. (A.R.Packer)

J. Laurie's ex-RTL51, seen in its operator's home town of Hamilton on 17th April, clearly displays the fleetname used by the business. A direction indicator has been fitted using the London Transport semaphore holder as a base. Continuing its previous owner's high standards of maintenance, the bus had been commendably well altered and repainted. (A.J.Douglas)

Negotiating a roundabout in the centre of Hanley on 28th May, ex-RT1407 is painted in the dark green and cream livery of T.Beckett of Bucknall, an independent operator later taken over by Potteries Motor Traction. A clutter of road signs spoils the efforts of the local authority to brighten up the neighbourhood. (A.R.Packer)

Negotiating Donegall Square in Belfast, former D37 is en-route to Holywood Road. The bus carries a sticker in the front lower deck saloon window reading 'Special Car 8d maximum fare'. The term 'car' is a strangely provincial one, redolent of tramway operation. The chassis of Belfast Corporation fleet number 460 is a CWA6 model, the W standing for its wartime build date although it gave over twenty-five years service before eventual withdrawal in November 1970, confirming the durability of products built by Transport Vehicles (Daimler) Ltd., the bus section of this respected marque. (D.F.Parker)

With the roundabout at the junction of the A41 trunk road and Spur Road in the background, Cricklewood garaged RT3359 exchanges passengers on its Route 142 journey to Watford Junction. The arches, which can be seen above the traffic waiting to negotiate the roundabout, would have carried the proposed Northern Line extension to the so-called 'Bushey Heath' had not the Second World War intervened. (R.Wellings)

1946 built former B22 originally fitted with Duple bodywork received a new ECW example with slightly higher seating capacity in March 1955 while in the ownership of Brighton, Hove and District. The bus, which of course was regarded as non-standard in London, completed double the number of years operating on the south coast that it did within the capital, eventually being sold for scrap in July 1966. (Surfleet)

Since the overall height of an RLH was 13'3½" it could safely negotiate the Headstone Lane railway bridge with its headroom of 13'9". Over the years many standard height vehicles have come a cropper here. Continuing on its journey between Rayners Lane Station and Northwick Park Station by way of Route 230, the driver of Harrow Weald's RLH62 pulls out to give the cyclist a wide berth. (J.A.S.Hambley collection)

A batch of one hundred of the basic Leyland TD4 chassis mounted with bodies by Leyland themselves were the only pre-war double deck buses purchased by the LPTB not to use an AEC chassis. Both chassis and bodywork incorporated many detail changes and modifications to imitate the contemporary AEC with operator built bodywork numbered in the STL sequence then entering service during 1937. Former STD74, disposed of to W.North of Leeds in January 1955, was quickly acquired by Smith's Luxury Coaches Ltd. of Reading operating in passenger service until 1958. Later converted to open top for further use as a service vehicle it is seen here with the owner's emblem still in place while parked beside their garage premises. Disposed of to a showman in 1961 it was last sighted and reported in 1964. (J.A.S.Hambley collection)

On 2nd July the 05.31 departure of night route 296 from Waterloo is being worked by RT3881 which, prior to its April 1959 overhaul, was painted green and operated in the northern Country Area. The 296 route, which originated in 1933 as the 613, ploughed a rather lonely furrow in the 1960 night network. It ran across Waterloo Bridge, along Fleet Street then turned up Farringdon Street to Rosebery Avenue and thence via the erstwhile 581 trolleybus route to Leyton. By so doing it catered for the Fleet Street print workers and the Mount Pleasant postmen. (A.R.Packer)

RM124 parked at the Minories bus and coach station, Aldgate, is highlighted with shadows falling from the electric infrastructure still required to maintain the operation of trolleybus route 653. The use of route number 48 in stage 4 of the trolleybus conversion programme on 11th November 1959 had been made possible with the withdrawal of the Cannon Street to West Norwood route in August 1958. The Saturday and Sunday service on the new route terminated at Aldgate while the Monday to Friday daytime operation continued through the City to Waterloo. Note the advertising for the British Rail Starlight Special service between London, Edinburgh and Glasgow highlighting the cost as a mere 85/- (£4.25)! (John A.S.Hambley collection)

Monday to Saturday Route 29A was introduced during 1955 to operate between Oakwood Station and Victoria although by the time RTL1622 was pictured, the route had become more localised, operating only from Oakwood Station to Turnpike Lane Station. It would be renumbered 298A in September 1968. The bus is one of those immediately put into storage on delivery in October 1954 not entering service until March 1958, some two months after some of the earlier members of the class had been sold. (J.A.S.Hambley collection)

Parked inside the old Amersham & District garage, GS75 is kept company by GS52 both waiting their call for further service on one of the several small capacity bus routes operated in the area. The subject vehicle would eventually be one of the many GSs owned by B.S.Williams Ltd. (Southern Motorways) of Emsworth, Sussex. This one completed six year's service before eventual disposal to James, a dealer of Botley, Hampshire for scrap. (D.F.Parker)

In this view on 24th June the driver of Mortlake's RTL89 is in the process of changing the destination blind before departure on a further Route 9 journey after his bus has been curtailed at Hammersmith. 'Bank' was possibly the shortest destination on London Transport blinds but it was seldom used in practice. (A.R.Packer)

RT2774 has been overhauled since its appearance on page 14 of the 1956 book of this series and here it waits at Watford Junction prior to departure to Ruislip Lido on Route 158. The previous body carried, numbered 6273, had been replaced on its visit to Aldenham in October 1959 by an earlier example, number 2103, both having been built by Park Royal Vehicles. It is interesting to see that a complete set of direction indicators are fitted to this bus which also carried an HD garage stencil plate, while RT2869 in the background, overhauled a month later, requires further work to complete the addition of its 'ears'. (A.Mortimer)

Standing at the weekday Finsbury Square, Moorgate terminal of Route 21 sometime in July, RT311, now with its home garage code NX painted on the bodywork, waits departure for Sidcup Garage. The year under review witnessed the Central Area bus fleet discard garage stencils in favour of the cheaper method of painting the garage code on the buses. It was another four or five years before the Country Area followed suit. Advertising for drivers and conductors on the two front panels includes the slogans 'It's a good job' and 'It's a service', words that regrettably in the main buck current attitudes. (A.R.Packer)

The trolleybuses, like K2 class number 1336 on Route 649, turned back at Liverpool Street with a U-turn in Bishopsgate. The 557 trolleybus route from Chingford Mount would have performed a similar manoeuvre but replacement bus route 257 has worked through from London Bridge Station, a much more useful and practical terminus. To the left of the picture and above the prominent keep left bollard is the warning sign 'Trolley Bus Turn' just in case the layout of the wires had not been noticed. RM243 had entered service at Walthamstow in April of the year under review, a little under twenty-one years since the trolleybus made its debut. (M.Rooum)

Route blinds which simply read 'TOWN SERVICE' were introduced in the new towns mushrooming within the Country Area sphere of operations during this period. With new estates springing up at such a pace, routes were often diverted or extended to meet the needs of the burgeoning population and this saved the expense of producing frequent new blind sets. Twice during the year under review Welwyn Garden City route 324 was altered although basically it continued as a circular operation from Knightsfield via the town centre and Heronswood Road as depicted by RTL1278. This bus station is now covered by the Howard Shopping Centre while in the background the signal box on the East Coast main line is a thing of the past. (A.Mortimer)

RT2164 waits crewless at Barking before a journey north to Chigwell Row, Maypole Inn on Route 62A. This was the Sunday version of Route 62 and on 7th February it had lost its horseshoe configuration, being cut back from Little Heath at Barking Broadway and re-routed via Upney Lane. The RT in this picture was originally one of a large number to first enter service at Nunhead garage during May and June 1949 replacing pre-war buses initially on Route 12. Serving the capital for nearly thirty years it finally succumbed to the demolition gangs of the Wombwell Diesels Company in April 1978. (J.A.S.Hambley collection)

Having completed a Sunday journey on Route 14, RTW130 from Chelverton Road, Putney garage rests amid the afternoon shadows falling in Cromwell Road, Kingston before resuming service to Hornsey Rise. In its present form the bus carries body number 3145, originally fitted to RTW245, while the chassis once provided the basis of RTW121 with further changes to take place before disposal in February 1966. Parked against the building is a Ford Prefect E493A in production between 1949 and 1953. (R.F.Mack)

A good view of RFW4 shows the front hinged saloon door in its open position while the inspector/courier assists passengers off the coach presumably at the end of their day out. Parked beside the Victoria Coach Station in Buckingham Palace Road an approaching Vauxhall Victor II car has a clear road in which to pass the coach. With no destination indicator equipment fitted to the class of fifteen vehicles the label attached within the upper portion of the nearside windscreen reading 'Windsor Hampton Court Tour' professionally accounts for the use of this coach. (R.H.G.Simpson)

Bexleyheath garaged RT4263 stands at the Parsons Hill, Woolwich terminal of Route 195 and its next journey will be a short working to Bexleyheath Market Place. Originally entering service in December 1950 with a Saunders built body, this fleet number continued in use until disposed of to Wombwell Diesels for scrap in May 1973. (K.Lane)

On 17th May 1959 Route 77A had been diverted on Sundays via Westminster Bridge and Lambeth Palace Road instead of Millbank and Lambeth Bridge and consequently renumbered 77C. Camberwell garage's Sunday allocation on the 77 group of routes is demonstrated by RTL1397 which is well laden as it traverses Woburn Place. It is interesting to note the parking allowed in the middle of the road, something only permitted to taxis nowadays while in the far distance two coaches are parked on the forecourt of the Royal National Hotel. (Photobus)

STL2093 first entered passenger service garaged at Cricklewood in June 1937. Initially the chassis carried STL15 bodywork but in April 1949 an STL16 type body, number 91, was fitted. Disposed of in June 1955 to W.North of Leeds, it soon became the property of Reliance Motor Services (Newbury) Ltd. as their fleet number 39. It entered the preservation movement in May 1958 and today, although now in need of attention, is still part of the collection owned by the London Bus Preservation Trust and garaged at Cobham. This view of the bus was taken at a vintage rally held at Hatfield on 24th September of the year under review, only sixteen months into its prolonged life. Strangely it was fitted with blinds for Route 43, not a route regularly associated with the STL class. (J.Firth)

Stevenson of Uttoxeter acquired their first ex-London buses in April 1957, made up of RT1465, RT1466 and RTL270. The first of the trio is pictured on 5th August at the town centre terminal stand which required vehicles to reverse across the main road, aided by a whistle blowing conductor. Carrying fleet number 14, it is slowly boarded by passengers before departure on the main road route to Burton via Tutbury. Beside the RT stands an earlier acquisition, a former Burton Corporation Guy Arab III fitted with front entrance Brush bodywork. (A.J.Douglas)

Standing on the semi circular forecourt at the front of Uxbridge Station, which is now buried in a pedestrianised area, RF11 is en-route from Chesham to Godstone on Route 709 in this December view. After receiving an overhaul in March of the year now under review, the coach was only spasmodically seen on the streets of the capital, pressed into service to cover for deficiencies in standard RF coaches. Sold in February 1964 it saw further service with Premier Travel Ltd. of Cambridge and was later purchased by preservationists. Sadly however it was in due course reduced to scrap by P.V.S., the Carlton dealer. (A.R.Packer)

In this wintry scene with Golders Green Underground Station in the background, deserted RT2619 stands dressed for its next journey to London Bridge by way of Route 13. Having re-entered service at Hendon garage from an April 1959 overhaul, the bus would continue to carry its painted AE code until a further visit to works in March 1963. (D.F.Parker)

RTL524 en-route for Finsbury Park Station in September on Route 233 is about to depart the bus stop at the western end of Lordship Lane, Wood Green. Beyond the school of dancing and the cluttered timber yard is Redvers Road, the terminal stand for the Lordship Lane trolleybus routes by now reduced to just those running into town via Tottenham and Stamford Hill. The RTL had been unlicensed and out of use at Upton Park before its transfer to West Green garage in October 1958 some five months prior to Route 233 being converted to all double deck operation. (A.R.Packer)

En-route for Crystal Palace RT196 pauses at the long standing bus stop at The Pavement, Clapham Common on its lengthy 137 journey from Archway to Crystal Palace. The ancestry of this route can be traced back to the famous independent Route 536 between Archway and Beckenham Junction among other places which featured the fine machines of City and Birch in the early nineteen thirties. (A.Mortimer)

RT2335 had been outshopped from overhaul in April 1957 to re-enter service at Sutton garage until its next visit to Aldenham in October of the year under review. On 1st August it is seen working the Morden Station to Epsom Racecourse express service with passengers boarding from the grass verge at the Surrey racecourse. A policeman and London Transport inspector are ready to keep order among the, as yet, few members of the race-going public wishing to return home. (Pamlin Prints)

This charming photograph of ex-LT1000 in use as a caravan with its posed children and dog and adult peering from the interior could almost have come straight out of a family album. The print is dated 27th July, a mere nine months before this unusual vehicle was broken up on site at the picturesque Bosham village in Hampshire during April 1961. The experimental chassis built at Chiswick Works in 1930 was one of four to which were mounted 54 seat double deck bodies. In this view it is fitted with a Duple coach body which had been built for a chassis exhibited on the Tilling Stevens stand at the October 1937 Commercial Motor Show. Having been disposed of by the LPTB in August 1939 this unique vehicle managed a creditable twenty-two years with a variety of South coast owners before arriving at its last resting place. (J.A.S.Hambley collection)

Middle Row garaged RTL480, still carrying a pre-1956 style intermediate point blind for Route 28, stands in the forecourt of Golders Green station on 15th April soon to leave for Wandsworth Bridge. In the background two Stockwell RTLs - from left to right RTL741 and RTL1550 - are working Routes 2 and 2B respectively. It is interesting to note the patterned stone block service of this terminal still in place after several decades of use. (A.R.Packer)

At the specially constructed terminus at Highgate Village built for the tram to trolleybus conversion in 1939, RM385 waits departure to Moorgate, Finsbury Square on Route 271. This was the only Highgate depot trolleybus conversion involved with stage seven of the programme introduced on 20th July when Route 611 was replaced. In the background RM379 waits to enter the terminal while a white capped driver removes himself from the previous arrival. The enamel jug and bowl housed in the tiny inspector's hut are interesting. The inspector who is wearing gloves is hardly likely to get his hands dirty. (J.A.S.Hambley collection)

Route 301C was an off-shoot of the trunk route 301 and operated between Hemel Hempstead and the Durrants Farm Estate at Berkhamsted with a few journeys continuing to Tring. RT625 stands in Hemel Hempstead bus station before journeying north again. Following overhaul in November the bus would re-enter service at Garston garage never to return to Two Waters. In the future following a further overhaul it was to emerge from Aldenham Works in Central Area colours. (A.R.Packer)

During its twelve years of passenger use with London Transport, RTL1163 was only officially garaged at two locations, firstly Wandsworth when the RTL class ousted RT operation in March 1951 and then Stockwell following its first overhaul in June 1955. Disposed of in July 1963 to Harding Coaches of London, SE1 for the intention of providing spares, it was later rescued by the preservation movement and its losses refitted. It enjoys continued existence having passed through several owners. In this 1960 scene it passes along the north side of Shepherds Bush Green on its long Sunday journey to Belmont Station, which it will reach in an hour and a half's time. (Photobus)

Purley Fountain is an apt name for the location of this photograph as RF178 splashes onwards through the sudden summer deluge as it journeys to East Grinstead on a 708 working. Anyone wishing to alight from a 109 or wait for a 234 at the marooned bus stop would have been in difficulties. The array of shop fronts is a reminder of days long since passed with such former household names as Gerrards the greengrocers and United Dairies for fresh dairy products together with the old style of J. Sainsbury store. (A.Mortimer)

RT1176 pulls clear of a parked lorry as it departs the bus stop sited beside the Purley branch of the National Provincial Bank on 19th November. Between overhauls received in May 1957 and June 1961 the bus was always officially allocated to Croydon garage which housed only RT double decks and a few single deck RFs for many years until the RM made its appearance for Route 64 on 1st February 1964. When delivered to London Transport in June 1949 Saunders bodywork was carried but here it carries a Park Royal example which had first seen service in January 1954 as RT4661. (A.R.Packer)

After overhaul in January of the year under review, RT2915 re-entered service at Forest Gate garage and is seen at Stratford Broadway en-route to Becontree Heath on Route 25 carrying G35 running plates. With the closure of the garage in connection with the sixth stage of the trolleybus conversion after operations on the night of 26th April the bus would be transferred to Upton Park along with eight others to cover the former Forest Gate workings on Routes 86 and 145. (A.Mortimer)

On 19th November Carshalton garaged RT3851 stands in Tamworth Road, Croydon with redundant trolleybus poles still in situ in the background some four months after they were last required. The bus now has Saunders bodywork in place of the non-roof box variety manufactured by Weymann carried when it first entered service in October 1950 at Wandsworth. Front corner panel advertising announces the latest Elvis Presley film 'G.I.Blues'. (A.R.Packer)

From left to right, RMs 262, 273, 258, 66, 238, 317 and RT1822 with two further unidentified RTs are seen inside West Ham garage soon after the completed transformation from trolleybus operation. The depot had been involved with motor bus operation from the fourth stage of the replacement programme. This was followed by further involvement with stage five leading to total motor bus operation with stage six on 27th April of the year under review. Also on this date Forest Gate garage closed and their RTs used on Route 25 were transferred into the revamped West Ham premises resulting in this mixed fleet. (K.V.Partridge)

Having reversed earlier into a suitable empty space at St. Mary's Square, Hitchin, long before the introduction of bay markings and bus only signs, RT1066 provides better and more comfortable seating than that occupied by the woman who keeps an eye on the photographer. The forthcoming journey to New Barnet Station on Route 303 on 27th August will take this green liveried bus from the northern extremity of the Country Area to the northern extremity of the Central Area. (A.R.Packer)

Viewed inside Shepherds Bush garage, which was rebuilt in the 1950s, RM395 waits further use, having previously arrived on a garage journey off Route 268 with the customary Wells Road destination blind. The background is filled with other members of the RM class together with a Leyland RTL, a type with which the garage had been associated since 1949. The combination of the bodywork and frame assemblies which last carried the fleet number of this RM can now be found in the U.S.A., which country together with Canada has seen a reasonable influx of the class for various uses. (J.Gascoine)

RM76 waits departure at Stratford Broadway to East Ham, White Horse carrying stencil WH plates rather than the painted garage code now used throughout the Central Area bus fleet. Following delivery in September 1959 the bus had spent much time unlicensed or on learner duties until late in the year now under review it had finally entered regular passenger service. Introduced on 3rd February, Route 272 part replaced the circular 689/690 trolleybuses although it wasn't until October 1961 that the circular operation was reintroduced, albeit a little different to the erstwhile trolleybus operation.

(J.A.S.Hambley collection)

En-route for the small community of Downside south of Cobham village, TD90 with a rather diminutive driver carries a respectable number of passengers. Approaching traffic lights as indicated by the rubber padded sensor in the road, the black and white pole on the pavement carries details of the 1960 style parking restrictions. The bus would complete its passenger use at Kingston garage, having initially entered service in May 1949 at the same location. In the intervening years Muswell Hill, Leyton and North Street, Romford garages had used the bus for varying periods. (Photomatic)

At Walthamstow RM154 passes the sports grounds close to the Crooked Billet. Route 257 had commenced operation on 3rd February with the fifth stage of the trolleybus replacement programme, the bus also entering passenger service on the same date garaged at Walthamstow. (A.Mortimer)

Ex-STL2683, now in the ownership of Widnes Corporation, shows off its red and cream livery while on a service to Halebank via St. Michaels. A total of four of these 18STL20s had been acquired by the Corporation through Norths, the Leeds dealer, in August 1955. They entered service in the same month carrying fleet numbers 22 to 25. By the end of 1962 all had been withdrawn from service with three securing a further lease of life, albeit only as huts, while the bus shown carrying fleet number 23 would be the odd one out being scrapped immediately after withdrawal. (J.A.S.Hambley collection)

This panoramic view of Epsom Downs clearly gives an idea of the large open space available for visitors to the race meetings. RT1401 is operating on the Express service between Morden and the racecourse on 1st August. While the Thornton Heath Garage on its destination blind might help the driver find his bus among all the other RTs, it is a little confusing to the passengers who will be disembarked on arrival at Morden. (Pamlin Prints)

While on private hire duties on 6th October, RFW1 is seen parked and deserted at Battersea Wharf. Delivered as one of the fifteen eight feet wide vehicles together with the 7'6" wide RF1 to RF25 during 1951, just in time for the Festival of Britain, they replaced the tired LTC and solitary TF9 private hire coaches. The entire complement of forty vehicles was sold by January 1965 following London Transport's withdrawal from this field of activity. After a short period with Elm Park Coaches Ltd. of Romford this coach gave several years service to St. Thomas' Hospital in London finally being scrapped by Wombwell Diesels in May 1970. (J.H.Aston)

At Aldgate during December RTL127 departs down Minories with a light load of passengers for Camberwell Green via Tower Bridge. This route employed a 'lazy' blind display for many years leaving passengers to guess which way the route went from Tower Bridge to Camberwell. From February 1949 to December 1963 this bus was only officially garaged at Barking, Riverside and Camberwell from where it was withdrawn. (A.R.Packer)

During the first week of new route 268, introduced on 20th July as a replacement for trolleybus services 626 and 628, RM355 works duty S 11. The trolleybuses of course had come from Hammersmith Depot but the replacement motor buses were provided from Shepherds Bush garage. This particular RM was transferred the following month to Elmers End and a further transfer to Thornton Heath took place in May 1962. The location is Putney Bridge Road, nearing the West Hill junction at Wandsworth, and the trolleybus wiring has been left in place for the 655 which would be withdrawn in November, allowing all trace of electric traction along this stretch of road to be removed. (D.Berwick)

RT3935 originally carried a Weymann built body but with its overhaul in June 1958 it was outshopped with one of the three hundred Saunders manufactured examples. It is seen at West Croydon on 19th November en-route to Raynes Park by way of Route 157. This was the last day for the event advertised on the side of the bus but Haigs are already looking to a little Xmas comfort. (A.R.Packer)

Ex-private hire RF22, now the Victoria garage based emergency vehicle, has been brought out as a substitute for a Route 707 coach to Oxted and is seen on Eccleston Bridge. It has a reduced destination display to enable most Green Line routes and basic destinations to be included and carries a side board with the simple 'Green Line' fleet name. During August 1962 it was demoted to learner duties followed by disposal to the Ilford dealer, Aspec Travel in May 1963. From the fact that it has not fully retracted, it is interesting to note that the semaphore trafficator is still in situ. (J.A.S.Hambley collection)

As a result of an allocation of RM buses on trial at Turnham Green garage during October 1959 a handful of RTs were either delicensed or transferred elsewhere including RT699. Carrying the AB Twickenham garage code, the shirt sleeved driver waits for two bells at Butterwick bus station on a Sunday in June before leaving on a shortened run on Route 90C to Richmond Bridge, the terminus for garage bound journeys. (A.R.Packer)

Leyton garaged RT2300 rests at the Green Man, Leytonstone although rather oddly the destination blind is showing 'Leytonstone, Harrow Green', which is just under a mile down the road. A long time resident of the east London garage, the bus even returned after an overhaul in February 1957 having initially arrived in August 1953 and it did not depart until April 1961. This is only part of the story since it was in August 1949 that RT2300 first entered service at Dalston garage, not departing London Transport ownership until October 1976, a glorious 27 plus years of service to the capital's inhabitants. (A.Mortimer)

In the route changes introduced at Stage 4 of the trolleybus conversion programme the existing route 23 had been strengthened and a Poplar allocation of RM added. RM96 had previously been used in passenger service trials operating from Turnham Green garage before its transfer during February of the year under review to the former East End trolleybus depot. With destination blind showing Poplar, Aberfeldy Street it stands on road setts near to its home base.
(J.A.S.Hambley collection)

December 1953 saw GS buses garaged at Guildford enter service on the 448 and 448A routes operating from Onslow Street Bus Station to Ewhurst or Pewley Way. GS66 is seen within its home town, closely followed by a RF. On 12th August 1964 Route 448 and its town offshoot 448A passed in their entirety to Tillingbourne Valley Motor Services whose origins on this route go back to 1924. Joint operation with London Transport had been co-ordinated ever since July 1935 although it was not until after 1964 that the Tillingbourne company displayed the 448/448A numbers. (J.A.S.Hambley collection)

RT3423 is seen in busy Watford town centre on a 318A short journey terminating at Garston garage. The full cross-town service operated a U shaped route from the rather remote Bucks Hill, situated between Chipperfield and Sarratt. Traversing minor roads through to Croxley, the service then passed through heavily populated Watford and its northern outskirts to terminate at Hazelwood Lane, Abbots Langley. (A.Mortimer)

The five hundred strong fleet of eight feet wide RTW class vehicles were affectionately known either as the 'fat ladies' or 'ballrooms' by certain quarters of the road transport fraternity. At Butterwick, Hammersmith on 25th June RTW6 in this picture somehow makes its extra six inches look much more. The front corner advertising which almost fits the available width and the thick black rubber mouldings to the indicator box both contribute to their uniqueness. It is said that they had particularly heavy steering and a day's work on the busy and somewhat tortuous Route 11 could be a tiring experience. (A.R.Packer)

With around two years public service still to complete before starting its later role as a staff bus, T787 stands at the Pound Hill South terminal of Route 853 some twelve years after first entering service at Leavesden Road garage, Watford. Route 853 had been introduced in 1955 as a Crawley New Town service, ploughing several different furrows between Three Bridges, Manor Royal and Pound Hill, eventually being withdrawn after operation on 1st December 1967. The bus was used by Henry James, a contractor of Mansfield after sale by London Transport but eventually disappeared, presumably to the scrapyard. (J.A.S.Hambley collection)

Initially entering service at Norwood garage in November 1950, RT4255 departed for its second overhaul in September 1958, re-entering service at Potters Bar. On 9th July it is seen at Victoria Station waiting to depart on a short working to Muswell Hill Broadway. The base of the old control tower can be seen at the right of the photograph although the tower itself and the lights it once controlled have now disappeared. (A.R.Packer)

Route 307B operated on Saturdays only between Hemel Hempstead bus station and Chaulden, Lower Sales situated on the outskirts of the town, a distance of a mile as the crow flies. The use of double deck RT3815 for this particular duty during October appears justified judging by the passengers who have boarded. The blind arrangement looks to have been rather hastily conceived although a proper display was available as can be seen in the 1961 book of this series. (A.R.Packer)

Standing on the forecourt of the Piccadilly Line Alperton Station, RTW227 waits departure on a short working of Route 46 to Willesden garage which was the evening and Saturday p.m. terminal, rather than Waterloo which was served at other times. For a few days in July 1950 the bus had temporarily been used in service at Willesden garage in connection with one of the eight feet wide bus trials conducted on inner London routes. It returned to the garage seven years later to complete its final years of operation before being withdrawn in April 1965. (A.Mortimer)

Setting out on its journey to Hayes Station on Route 204, RT3336 negotiates the roundabout in Bakers Road, which is more commonly described as Uxbridge bus station. The 204, nowadays called U4, commenced in July 1951 breaking hitherto unserved roads between the two termini. The long December shadows shroud Garston garaged RT4551 in the background working on Route 321. (A.R.Packer)

RT4640 of Seven Kings garage with seated crew in the lower saloon, rests at Ilford between journeys on the twenty minute long weekday working of Route 129. A Sunday extension to Little Heath added another quarter of an hour to the through journey. First entering service in December 1953 with Park Royal bodywork, the bus gained an older example from the same stable on its first overhaul but this has since been replaced by a Weymann product on a further visit to Aldenham earlier in the year under review. Eventually disposed of for scrap in July 1976 it had by that time once again reverted to bodywork from the original source. (M.Rooum)

The Sunday allocation of Routemasters on Route 9 from Poplar garage is exemplified by RM102 as it pauses in Butterwick at Hammersmith on its journey to Mortlake on a sunny Sunday in September. The Hammersmith Depot trolleybus routes have now been replaced by RMs working from Shepherds Bush garage and so the nearside set of wires which led to the depot have been removed. For the time being however the other set remain intact for the 655 route which will be removed in November. (A.R.Packer)

Route 142 worked between Watford Junction and Kilburn Park Station on weekdays, only running to Edgware Station on Sundays. RT750 of Edgware garage works the route in this picture, the bus first entering service at Dalston in July 1948. It operated in Central Area livery until September 1963 when, after overhaul, it re-entered service in Country Area green which it carried until sale in October 1970 after ten months in the ownership of London Country Bus Services. (A.Mortimer)

RM111 leaves Bloomsbury on 2nd July on the 06.10 departure for the garage at Poplar, Aberfeldy Street as it finishes its night's work on Route 284. The bus had been transferred to Poplar garage in November 1959 at the same time as this new night route was introduced, basically between Poplar and Trafalgar Square with one journey working to and from Barking. It had replaced the night journeys on trolleybus 665. Turnham Green garage had been the first to use this RM in passenger service from 1st November 1959, when it was the highest numbered used in the trial service programme. (A.R.Packer)

Prior to its purchase by the Garelochhead Coach Services of Dumbarton in June 1961, as depicted on page 14 of the 1962 book of this series, ex-RT1480 had already been used in service by two other operators since disposal by the Executive in April 1956. East Midland Motor Services of Chesterfield had acquired the business of Wass Brothers Ltd. of Mansfield on 1st April 1958 whose fleet of ten vehicles included three Craven bodied RTs. Numbered by East Midland D45 to D47 they were used in service until late 1960, all being disposed of to F.Cowley, the Salford dealer, in January 1961. Seen in rain soaked Mansfield town centre on 12th May of the year under review, a few passengers have availed themselves of the Route 10 bus for a journey to Manton or Gateford. (R.Holmes)

In the vicinity of South Croydon garage two route number roof box RTs of differing classification travel south on their respective routes with glorious weather prevailing on this particular Sunday. To the left of the picture RT2337 is soon to make a left hand turn into the garage having completed its Route 12 journey. RT1137 on the other hand will finish rather further to the south at its Chipstead Valley terminal. (N.Rayfield)

A workman loads the 6½ ton lorry 447W, while in the background some members of the 'pre-war' RT class await their fate in this, the year when the greatest number were disposed of. In the immediate foreground to the left an unwanted request bus stop flag lays among an assortment of rubble. The chassis of the lorry had originally been fitted with 27-seat bodywork of coach standards entering service in September 1930 as T171. Rebodied for its new role in August 1940 it was to last until April 1961 before being disposed of the W.North of Leeds and reduced to scrap before the year end. (J.Lines collection)

At the *Weybridge* terminal of Route 461A, RT4536 waits in early spring sunshine before commencing a journey to Botleys Park, St. Peter's Hospital. This green liveried RT had originally been fitted with the body of SRT84 and remained in Country Area livery until its final visit to Aldenham when an RT4536 re-entered service at Norbiton garage in the red colour scheme. (A.Mortimer)

Morden Underground station forecourt provides the resting place for RT2552 before it departs on a journey to Tattenham Corner Station on Route 164A with duty plates A30. The bus had returned from its March 1959 overhaul having gained an early Park Royal body, number 1588. Ayrshire Bus Owners (A1) Services acquired the bus direct from London Transport in November 1963 and managed to obtain a further two years service from it before it was scrapped in January 1966. (A.R.Packer)

Ex-G151 was scrapped in 1962 by Dunsmore, a Larkhall dealer, having been in London passenger use and then Perth during its operational years which had commenced in July 1945. This 56 seat Park Royal bodied Guy Arab bus was disposed by London Transport in March 1953 to W.Alexander & Sons, later operating for Alexander (Midland). Seen in Perth City centre on 5th March in its current operator's livery, little, apart from the rebuilt blind box and a Guy nameplate on the radiator, alter its previous appearance. (A.J.Douglas)

RF359, with what nowadays would be a cherished registration, initially entered service in December 1952 at Bromley garage. After varying lengths of time spent at a number of garages it would end its career at Uxbridge in December 1976 to be disposed of in the following February. From May 1959 through to March 1961 it was allocated to Norbiton and here in December it waits at Hampton Court Station before departing on a journey to Kingston by way of the circuitous route 201. A Morris Traveller is parked on the right with the wood framing so typical of this type of car in the period. (A.R.Packer)

At the sleepy village of Turners Hill, West Sussex London Transport's RF613 en-route for Edenbridge on the long 434 route meets up with Southdown Motor Services' EUF171 on Service 38 bound for Haywards Heath. While the RF dates from July 1953 the Southdown vehicle is considerably older being a 1938 built Leyland Titan which had been rebodied by East Lancs in 1947. The village store appears to be closed so it could have been a Sunday or perhaps an early closing day. (R.Hobbs)

Craven bodied ex-RT1482 now in the ownership of Red Rover, Aylesbury, is seen parked within the town centre on a snowy 16th January with a former City of Oxford AEC Regal, registered NJO713 to keep it company. Before its untimely withdrawal from service due to accident damage in September 1962, the RT had become something of a celebrity. It appeared in two Elstree Studios films, firstly 'The Young Ones' followed by 'The Pot Carriers' disguised as a London bus. (A.R.Packer)

RTL1588 had been transferred from Clayhall to Athol Street, Poplar garage in November 1959 maintaining an association with the East End of London which was to continue after the closure of the Athol Street garage on 10th May 1961 when it moved to nearby Poplar. Standing outside the Athol Street premises the RTL is dressed for a positioning journey to 'Stepney Direct' for duty on Route 82 from Stepney to Rotherhithe, St. Mary Church Street. The buildings, which previously occupied the site on the left hand side of the picture, had been demolished some years earlier and bombing raids during World War II had devastated much of the surrounding area. Nowadays it is extremely difficult to identify just where this garage was; such has been the re-development. (A.Mortimer)

One of the few GSs which has not so far been portrayed in this series of books, GS53 of Northfleet heads through the streets of Gravesend on its journey to the White Swan at Ash. Beginning and ending its passenger service at this Kentish garage, the bus was later used by the Chesham Youth Club and then the Inns of Court and Gainsford Boys Club of London W.C.2 before disappearing from history while with an unidentified owner in Essex in the early 1970s. (D.A.Ruddom collection)

After disposal to the dealer, Bird's Commercial Motors, in May 1956, ex-RT1438 was acquired two months later by H.Brown, trading as Garelochhead Coach Services. McGills Bus Services Ltd. of Barrhead became the vehicle's third operator in February 1960 and used the bus in passenger service for a comparable number of years to its first owners. On 29th May it is seen at Barrhead finished in its latest highly reflective paint scheme with only an overspill of diesel fuel to mar its appearance. (A.J.Douglas)

The Ionic portico of St. Pancras New Church, completed in 1822 and the most expensive church of its time, makes an impressive background to New Cross garage's RT1332. The driver's attention seems to be distracted by some problem or other as he prepares to pull away from the bus stop. Route 188 had been born with Stage 4 of the tram conversion programme on 11th July 1951 when buses from Peckham replaced the 68 tram route between Greenwich and Waterloo and continued north to Chalk Farm. By 1960 however the Sunday operation was handled by New Cross garage as shown here. Note the impossibility of mounting a Saunders built body on to an RTL chassis because of the continuing downward slope of the bottom line to the driver's cab front towards the dumbiron, clearly visible in this picture. (Photobus)

At the Sloane Square terminal of the Battersea Pleasure Gardens shuttle service 137A, RT4089 of Norwood garage has been rather awkwardly parked on a road junction. The only entry for this route in the 'red timetable' used by staff says 'Buses will be operated according to the requirements of traffic, and necessary journeys will be arranged locally by the Road officials'. Presumably the journey isn't necessary at this particular moment. (J.A.S.Hambley collection)

The original body and chassis combinations were retained throughout on the twenty-five private hire batch of RF vehicles. On private hire duty, Leyton's RF15 in all over green livery is seen with all the quarter drop windows in an open position. Withdrawn from service in September 1963 it was stored unlicensed until sold in December 1963. (R.H.G.Simpson)

Three night routes served Liverpool Street in 1960 with all venturing westward to their respective destinations using the Ludgate Hill, Fleet Street, Strand corridor to depart the environs of the City. RT3314 on 11th June waits departure for a journey on Route 294 to its home garage, while from the shadows of the awning provided by the tobacconist an inspector emerges with a querying expression on his face. The ABC teashop, still around in 1960, seemed to the author to be a little less sophisticated than its rival, 'Joe' Lyons. (A.R.Packer)

In its first summer of passenger operation, RM153 is parked at Moorgate, Finsbury Square while working Route 256. This had been introduced with stage 5 of the trolleybus replacement programme on 3rd February being a hybrid replacement for the northern section of the 685 trolleybus route which also provided new links into the City via the Millfields estate at Clapton. Upon its entry into service the bus was one of ninety which received the classification 5/5RM5/5. (J.A.S. Hambley collection)

Conflicting styles of architecture with the modern lines of the Granada cinema comparing favourably with the rear of the terraced dwellings in the vicinity of Clapham Junction set the scene for a Route 19 bus on its way to Highbury Barn from Upper Tooting. RTL1298, in the early stages of being fitted with trafficator ears, proceeds across the bridge over the railway on St John's Hill. The Metropolitan Police have decreed a no parking area, no doubt since the buses appear to be on a diversion from their normal routeing. Beyond another RTL, this time on Route 77, follows. (F.W.Ivey)

Thornton Heath's RT3996 en-route for Whyteleafe by way of Route 115 is forced by parked cars to stop some distance from the kerbside as it picks up passengers in Purley. The 115 service worked a curious horseshoe shaped route running from Wallington in a northerly direction to Mitcham and Streatham before turning back on itself down the main A23 to Croydon Airport just a mile and a half distant from where it had commenced before continuing on weekdays to Purley and Whyteleafe. (A.R.Packer)

RT746 was transferred from Merton to Camberwell garage during January only to be further transferred to Peckham during February. During its brief residence at Camberwell it is seen departing Clapham for Highams Park Station by way of Route 35 with a hopeful further passenger in hot pursuit. New Year sale shoppers eagerly view the offerings in the window display of Manny Harris Ltd., who describe themselves over the door as 'Clapham's Wool Headquarters'. Presumably they kept their sheep on Clapham Common! (A.Mortimer)

Seen in Hanley on 28th May en-route for Leek by way of F.Proctor of Bucknall's route 16, ex-RT1452 wears that operator's blue and cream livery. It had been acquired via Bird's Commercial Motors in June 1956 and would complete more years in passenger service in the Potteries then it did with London Transport but after seven years it was finally withdrawn from service and despatched for scrap. (A.R.Packer)

Sometime during July and waiting for departure time to arrive, RT3756 stands beside the Wimbledon Greyhound Stadium at Summerstown. The pre-decimal admission prices, which included a race card, translate to an almost unbelievable 25p, 15p and 50p. Route 64 had been extended to this terminal from West Croydon as part replacement for trolleybus 630 on 20th July. This rather obscure destination was mainly a matter of finding a convenient stand at which to lay over and in May the following year the route was cut back to Tooting Broadway. (D.Berwick)

Weekend operations in Hatfield were rather different to the rest of the week and one of the anomalies on Saturday and Sunday was the 341A route which ran from Marshalswick to South Hatfield. On 6th February of the year under review it was given a short extension at the latter point from Hazel Grove to Northdown Road and it is to this destination that RTL1276 is heading. As with all the green liveried RTLs their short Country Area passenger use was followed with demotion to learner duties, being the first large-scale use of the class in this category. (A.Mortimer)

RT2738 carries the Park Royal body number 2044 that it received in September 1959. It is waiting departure at North Woolwich for a further Route 101 journey to Manor Park Station and would remain at Upton Park garage until disposed of in September 1964 when it was exported to the Ceylon Transport Board. (A.Mortimer)

RTW315 stands at Victoria Station working a rather unusual short journey to Waterloo only, although in another eight years time this will be the full journey of Red Arrow Route 503. Recent heavy rain has subsided allowing pedestrians to go about their business once again, suitably dressed for any further sudden showers. Part of the character of the main station entrance has been destroyed with the removal of the various exotic destinations once carried along the canopy. (D.F.Parker)

Delivered during August 1954, green liveried RT4544 was immediately put into store at Loughton garage until required for service at Grays in May 1955. The chassis was mounted with Park Royal body number 3494 repainted from its original red colour scheme, having previously seen service as SRT160 on the chassis of ex-STL2438. The RT received its first overhaul in June 1959 and emerged from works fitted with Weymann body number 6919. Although overhauled again in March 1963 the bus was seriously damaged in an accident in August 1964 causing premature withdrawal and eventual disposal in March 1965 to F.Ridler of Whitton, Middlesex. On 26th June in happier times it stands beside Dartford garage fitted for a local duty on Route 477A to Joyce Green Hospital. (P.J.Malsher)

Two RF coaches grow colder in this wintry scene at Aylesbury on 16th January with well compacted snow on the pavement as a hazard to the unwary pedestrian. Safely seated passengers wait a journey on RF218 with front blind and route board in place for its long haul to Westerham via Route 706. The similar coach parked closely behind will follow thirty minutes later on Route 707 to Oxted. (A.R.Packer)

Night routes 284 - 292 and 294 - 299 were renumbered N84 - N92 and N94 - N99 on 28th September of the year under review, releasing the unprefixed numbers for further use, mainly in the remaining trolleybus replacement scheme. Recently overhauled RTL241 waits departure on 11th June from London Bridge station on one of the final two 289 journeys of the night to Hammersmith. These journeys were advertised as terminating at Shepherds Bush but the driver has set the blind to Hammersmith Broadway indicating the crew's willingness to carry passengers on the 'when working' section of the route to Riverside garage. (A.R.Packer)

The date is 16th April and RT1086 negotiates the climb up Bishops Rise on a 340B journey to South Hatfield, Southdown Road. In July this RT would be transferred to Windsor, being displaced by the green liveried RTLs seen elsewhere in this book. Many years later John Dengate and Son Ltd. of Rye in Sussex would operate the bus prior to its export to the USA. (P.J.Malsher)

Dalston's red liveried RLH57 finds itself in the unlikely town of Redhill on Route 447. During the year under review from April through to September it was on loan to Reigate garage who, in view of its colour, have added a slipboard on the bulkhead window which reads 'Green Rover Tickets are available on this bus, Red Rover tickets are not available'. Rather surprisingly the opportunity to fit trafficators was not taken at the time of its overhaul immediately prior to re-entering service on its six month loan to the Country Area. Leatherhead garaged RT1008 parked closely behind carries Kingston in the destination box for a 406 journey although the canopy blind displays 406A. (A.Mortimer)

Parked on the Walthamstow 'Crooked Billet' stand in Cecil Road RT2627, with destination blind showing Arnos Grove Station, waits departure on another journey on Route 34. In this view taken during February a RM lays over behind on the new 58 route which also terminated here. In April the 34 route would be extended down to Leyton as part of the next trolleybus conversion scheme. This RT would remain at Palmers Green garage for the rest of its passenger service until withdrawn in May 1964 whereupon it was immediately disposed of to Passenger Vehicle Sales of Ilford, Essex. (A.R.Packer)

Garston garaged RF581 clearly shows the new type of bright orange 'Pay As You Enter' slipboard introduced during 1960, which was an improvement on previous rather inconspicuous versions. It is working the Saturday afternoon route 322B which ran between Watford Junction and Kings Langley, The Nap via Kings Langley Station. This short-lived route was withdrawn after 21st May. The shoppers all seem to typify the ordered scene of 1960 and Hammond's photographic supply stores is as far as 'high tech' went in those days. (A.Mortimer)

RTW21 was garaged at Chalk Farm from May 1958 through to its withdrawal from public service in January 1966. Storage in delicensed condition followed at several garages prior to its disposal to the Ceylon Transport Board in December of the same year. Trolleybus overhead wiring is still in place in this September view and will remain so for another five months at this Hampstead Heath terminus. Blinds already set for its next journey on Route 24, the bus leans over as it turns left out of Fleet Road before being swung in the other direction to gain the stand behind the tree at South End Green. (A.R.Packer)

Bus Route 14 and trolleybus Route 639, two of the comprehensive range of services serving Kings Cross, converge for the short distance of common road which they shared. RTL931 from Chelverton Road, Putney garage is en-route for Kingston the Saturday destination of its route in 1960. Trolleybus 1412, an L3 class vehicle, is operating from Highgate Depot and was transferred to Fulwell in February 1961 with the 9th stage of the trolleybus conversion programme along with most of the depot's complement of the class. (Photobus)

Rogue workings of RTs from West Ham garage were not uncommon and in this instance RT1800 has been allocated to duty WH305 on the 41 route. The date is 12th November and the location a rather wet Stratford Broadway. Behind the bus the imposing St. John's Church can be seen together with the Martyrs' Memorial erected in Victorian times to commemorate eleven men and two women who were burnt at the stake for their Protestant beliefs on Stratford Green in 1556. (A.R.Packer)

GS71 stands in the Rickmansworth Station car park between trips on the 336A service provided basically for the residents of the private Loudwater Estate. The Garston bus used was outstationed on the estate and the driver/operator returned to Garston once a week to cash in and for refuelling and maintenance to the bus. GS operation on this not particularly busy route stretched from December 1953 through to 29th March 1972 easily making it the longest lasting served by the class. Several days before the route was finally withdrawn, transport enthusiasts supplemented the usual patronage to the extent that on the last day of operation two buses were in use to cope with the demand. (P.J.Malsher)

In the ownership of AA Motor Services of Ayr since June 1954, ex-D79, although still with its original Duple bodywork, had received a complete rebuilt during 1958 greatly improving its exterior appearance. Radiused corner saloon windows are housed in rubber mouldings while four sliding openings per side and redesigned front route blind boxes alter its London appearance. Chrome plated radiator shell and larger headlights give the bus a more stylish look than when in its original utility condition. In this 28th February view, both the cars which can be seen come from the Luton factory of Vauxhall Motors. (A.J.Douglas)

In Minories bus and coach station at Aldgate two RTs working Route 23 lay over before return to Becontree Heath. Nearest the camera RT2808 carries the Weymann RT3 body which initially entered service as RT570. Its Barking stable mate, RT2745, parked alongside also carries RT3 bodywork, this time by Park Royal, but it is one of the last 150 built which were later recoded RT10. Higher canopies, trafficator holders, upswept cab fronts to clear the larger Leyland dumbirons if necessary and bulkhead brackets to carry route number plates were distinguishing features of these bodies. (R.F.Mack)

The road surface at the Kings Cross junction is still finished with granite setts giving RTL1582, en-route to Roehampton on Route 30, a bumpy ride. The lack of activity suggests that this is a picture taken on a Sunday but today even the Sabbath would not provide such an uncluttered scene. (Photobus)

D177 had a fairly eventful life, first entering service at Romford, London Road garage in March 1946 on Green Line duties. When replaced by RT buses during 1950 it was transferred to Merton and received Central Area livery in the following year. Disposed of to W.North & Sons, the Leeds dealer, in April 1953 it was acquired together with two other examples by the White Bus Company of Bridlington. All three were taken over with the business by East Yorkshire Motor Services Ltd. in November 1955 but were never used in public service. This Daimler moved into showmen's ownership early in 1957. It is seen here at the 1960 Keighley Gala. Although still carrying its original Duple bodywork, most of the windows and the rear platform have been panelled over and signwriting is carried for J.Carvill & Son's Auto-Drome, which was a wall of death motorcycle ride. (T.Peart)

Operating between Wandsworth and Farringdon Street, night route 288 had been introduced on 1st October 1950 with the first stage of the post-war tram conversion programme. On 2nd July RTL1152 waits departure from Farringdon Street at 05.39 on the final journey of the night to Wandsworth garage. In the background RTL1404 on a daytime working of Route 168 to Putney Heath, Green Man will depart three minutes before the 288, following the same route as far as Vauxhall. (A.R.Packer)

Now in the ownership of W.Alexander & Sons, Falkirk, ex-G371 is seen in Perth City centre on 5th March being used on a service to Burghmuir. Cast plates fitted below the driver's windscreen carry fleet number RO 646 and Perth garage code in the good old traditional style of much of the provinces. Prior to the decision to divide the organisation in 1961, Alexander was one of the largest operators in the country. As a consequence of the break-up this Weymann bodied Guy Arab II continued in service as part of the initial Alexander (Midland) fleet. (A.J.Douglas)

Carrying Green Line colours and fleetname, RF19 is viewed at Uxbridge Station sometime in December undertaking more mundane work as a Country Area bus on Route 458. Commencing its comparatively short ownership with London Transport in May 1951 as a private hire coach and relegated to its new duties in October 1956 it would continue in service until withdrawn in July 1962. After its initial sale to Aspec Travel, a dealer in Ilford during June 1963 a very chequered career followed with threatened extinction on more than one occasion. Thankfully it entered the preservation movement six months short of its 30th birthday. (A.R.Packer)

The untidy advertising for newspapers, four of which – the Sunday Pictorial, Star, Daily Sketch and Daily Herald – are no longer with us, contrasts sharply with the tidy adverts carried by RTL641. Prior to receiving new RM class buses in July of the year under review, Shepherds Bush garage housed RTL class buses which it continued to do after taking on the former Hammersmith Depot trolleybus replacement routes. It was not surprising therefore to find RTLs occasionally in service on the routes which were intended for Routemaster operation. The bus pauses in Garratt Lane on its way to Harlesden, College Park, the normal terminal although Park Royal Stadium was reached during rush hours. (A.Mortimer)

Morden Underground station forecourt on a cold December afternoon provides the resting place for RT2331 between its journeys on the circular route 156, the direction of its next duty via Sutton & Cheam displayed on the destination blind. RT4431 standing on the right hand side of the picture will depart on a journey in the opposite direction as indicated on its blind. In the background is the imposing façade of the Odeon Cinema, currently showing the classic 'Around the World in 80 Days'. Perhaps the buses should have been branded 'Around Sutton and Cheam in 42 Minutes'. (A.R.Packer)

Wartime delivered G68, a Guy Arab Mark I with Park Royal bodywork for 56 passengers, saw service in the capital until disposed of to W.North & Sons, the Leeds dealer. It was acquired almost immediately by a showman who removed the upper deck bodywork above the bottom line of glazing and replaced the original roof. Other alterations to the exterior bodywork include panelling over all but the first saloon side window with the rear platform being attended to in similar fashion. Although not visible in this picture, the means of reaching the interior is now provided by an opening built into the rear. Looking well cared for it carries legal lettering reading 'N.Johnson, Featherstone'. (R.Wellings)

After the withdrawal of the Worcester Park to St. Helier route 32 in October 1956 the number was re-used starting in August 1959 for a rather hybrid invention running between Wanstead Station and Victoria in part replacement of the Bow Depot trolleybuses. RTL1282 appears to have turned short at Stratford before returning to Victoria. This RTL was transferred to Bow a few months before receiving an overhaul in November 1959. (A.R.Packer)

Between July 1958 and June 1961 Welwyn Hatfield town service 340B was extended on Saturdays to Hitchin to supplement the 303 service. Not long after their entry into service at Hatfield, one of the green liveried RTLs, 1264, heads through Hatfield New Town Centre on its way north. Unfortunately the conductor has not bothered to reset the via point blinds to cover the extension and 'Bishops Rise, South Hatfield' is not likely to be of much help once the bus leaves Hatfield. (A.Mortimer)

A large influx of RM buses entered service with the sixth stage of the trolleybus replacement programme on 27th April, which completed the conversion of both West Ham and Walthamstow depots. New routes 249 and 249A operated between Victoria and Albert Docks and the Royal Forest Hotel at Chingford replacing the 697 and 699 trolleybuses between the Docks and Chingford Mount. RM285 waits departure from Victoria and Albert Docks on a short working to Stratford in the upper picture while in the lower RM242 waits at Stratford before departing to the docks on a similar short working. In the latter case however it is a journey on the 249A schedule. Both views were taken on a somewhat wet 23rd December. (A.R.Packer)

Passing through Butterwick at Hammersmith, RT2539 and RTL130 have both only recently returned to service from their August overhauls. They now find themselves garaged at Turnham Green and Riverside respectively, both garages being convenient for the 27 route operation, although Turnham Green only had a Sunday commitment. The RT in the top picture is working the summer Sunday extension of the route to Hampton Court while in the lower picture the RTL is en-route to Richmond. Teddington Station was the normal daily terminal of this route with buses on shortened journeys to Richmond terminating at the station. The destination blind on this RTL appears to be using a Richmond, Lower Mortlake Road display which has been adapted to become generic to the area. (W.R.Legg / A.R.Packer)

RT118 had been used on revenue earning duties until the middle of 1955. It then became a staff bus and since September 1959 had been employed as a learner vehicle, initially at Croydon garage. Transferred to Barking in the spring of the year currently under review its condition has been allowed to continue to deteriorate and it stands beside land which appears to have suffered similar treatment. (J.A.S. Hambley collection)

RT3499 in its final form with body number 2249 rests in the St. Albans garage yard together with other RTs and RF595. A Green Line relief duty completed, running plates SA207 are still in place on the immaculately presented bus which has only recently returned to service from overhaul. The early roof box RT10 body (formerly classified RT3) led to its early sale and although it did find passenger service with other operators followed by promotional work it was scrapped in May 1971. (A.Mortimer)

Completely deserted of human contact, RF644 illustrates the unobtrusive entrance with the two folding saloon doors in the open position. A light fitted into the first step riser was complemented by a second situated at the front of the second riser illuminating this potentially hazardous area. Sufficient grab rails provide additional safety features for a class designed by London Transport with help from outside consultants for the first time, barring the solitary RTC coach produced some years earlier. The detailed minimum fare slipboard protects the less frequent and long distant 304 service from more local passengers in the St. Albans area. (A.Mortimer)

Resting at St. Mary's Square, Hitchin on Saturday 27th August, RT4787 displays route details for the Stevenage Town Service 801 and is destined for Longmeadow, a neighbourhood then on the south eastern extremities of development. The 801 in fact provided a regular half-hour service on Saturdays through to Hitchin at this time. Overhauled in June and returned to service at Stevenage, the lower panels show the muddy evidence of building work still in progress at Stevenage, which the Hatfield RT alongside has managed to avoid. The Stevenage bus was transferred to Grays in September, ending its only period of operation in the New Town. (A.R.Packer)

FXT427 had originally entered passenger service with London Transport fitted with Park Royal highbridge 56 seat bodywork as fleet number B9 in June 1942. It was withdrawn from London in June 1951. All nine of the small batch of wartime delivered buses with Bristol K5 chassis were intended to be purchased by Crosville Motor Service of Chester but one, ex-B5, entered service elsewhere. The eight operated by Crosville were all rebodied with either ECW or Strachan lowbridge bodywork of 1945 or 1948 manufacture with some receiving further rebodying in 1956. This bus with fleet number DKA168, seen here in Chester on 6th August, is an example which throughout its life has been fitted with three different bodybuilders products. (A.J.Douglas)

Despite the addition of some night routes following tram and trolleybus replacements, the night bus network in 1960 was still relatively sparse. Following its rapid expansion in the 1980s the trend nowadays is for night routes to match their daytime counterparts in both route and number. 297, which started running between Liverpool Street and Turnham Green in 1928 as 614 and in September of the year under review was renumbered N97 is one of the few that still survive today, although it now goes beyond Turnham Green to Heathrow Airport. In the cold light of a wet summer Saturday dawn on 11th June, RT507 waits departure from Liverpool Street to Turnham Green. (A.R.Packer)

Traversing Chingford Road on its journey to North Woolwich Free Ferry, RM60 is hotly pursued by a Hillman Husky car. The bus had first been used in passenger service from Poplar garage before being transferred to West Ham and except for two visits to Aldenham for overhaul would not venture further away until transfer to Dalston took place in November 1969. The front advertisements are for the then new Alfred Hitchcock film 'Rear Window' starring James Stewart, which has subsequently become something of a classic. (A.Mortimer)

Newly overhauled RTL70 departs the Wembley complex on private hire duties complete with AC (Willesden) garage plate. To the left of the picture 209UMX of Fountain Coaches and an RT family bus also head away to their respective destinations while an RT on Route 92 waits on stand for its departure time. (R.H.G.Simpson)

RT1019 stands at the Windsor Castle setting down point on Castle Hill. The destination blind has already been reset for a return journey to Uxbridge via Bangors Road North, which was the alternative route taken by the A variant of 457 at Iver Heath. The other unique feature of the 457A, travel via Upton Lea, is covered on the via point blind. After later service at Garston garage, this RT was disposed of in May 1964 and exported to Ceylon. (R.H.G.Simpson)

Nearing the end of its existence ex-T460 is seen on 19th April parked on open ground at Kilgetty, Carmarthenshire, in its final role as a gypsy caravan. With a protruding chimney stack and four neat structural struts added at roof level it still retains its unmistakable ancestry though nearing eighteen years since it last saw service in the capital. Its history between loan in November 1942 to the U.S. Forces stationed in England and its re-emergence in May 1946 with a Merthyr Tydfil registration remains one of those mysteries that will probably never be adequately resolved. (J.C.Gillham)

London Transport was very keen to promulgate the name 'Routemaster' for its new class of buses. The name was carried above the fleet number on both sides of new deliveries until October 1964 and transfers on the corner of the offside rear panel using the roundel to good effect were also carried by many examples as demonstrated by RM275. It is seen here at West Croydon on 23rd July bound for Wimbledon Stadium on Route 64. The now defunct overhead wiring is still in place and would soon be removed, not to return until 1999, albeit it in a different form, when Tramlink construction was under way. (Bespix)

Alongside a handy water can for thirsty radiators, Alperton's RT1735 attracts little attention at Edgware on Saturday 17th September. The blind is reset for its next journey to Bideford Avenue at Perivale on Route 79A. This RT only worked from Alperton garage between its September 1957 and August 1961 overhauls but its passenger service with London Transport stretched from May 1950 through to May 1976. The little door in the background leading to the rather ominous looking chimney bears the words 'This door is permanently locked', which rather defeats its purpose. (A.R.Packer)

1960 proved to be the most prolific in the use of the traditional single deck series of 200+ route numbers for new double deck services. On 20th July route number 220, unused since its demise in the Uxbridge area in January 1957, was re-introduced to the London scene. On the fourth day of the new route, which replaced trolleybus 630, RM394 negotiates the terminal loop at West Croydon with the now defunct wiring awaiting removal and the site subsequently developed into the West Croydon bus station standing empty. A Hillman Minx heads up Station Road in front of the bus. As in other pictures in this book, the well-behaved, immaculately dressed children holding their father's hands and the other pedestrians show what a different place 1960 London was to that experienced today. (Bespix)

In its temporary capacity as a learner vehicle, RM20 climbs Highgate High Street on a wet 7th July during its period in use from West Ham garage. However, since it is just three weeks before the Highgate Hill 611 trolleybus was converted it would be logical to assume it is training Highgate drivers on this occasion. In this role it was further used at Upton Park and Shepherds Bush garages before eventually entering passenger service during the last month of the year now under review. (Bespix)

Recently overhauled RT4273 stands at Stratford Broadway while substituting for a RM on Route 69 duty WH181. The fifth stage of the trolleybus conversion programme on 3rd February used the route number 69, which had been conveniently vacant since November 1958, to replace the 669 trolleybus. West Ham garage first received RTs in April 1960 when Forest Gate closed enabling odd workings such as this to occur. (A.Mortimer)

In 1960 the 334 route basically ran from either the Bus Station or Two Waters Garage to the Maylands Avenue Industrial Area in Hemel Hempstead with a few odd journeys to and from Gadebridge etc. Like all New Town routes its variations were manifold but in this instance it would seem that the 'Two Waters L.T.Garage' destination is a hangover from some previous trip since RT4772 stands alongside the Bus Station in Waterhouse Street. This was one of the vehicles put in store on delivery, only entering service in June 1959. (A.R.Packer)

RTL1299 is seen traversing Buckingham Palace Road and passing 'Airways House' with its BOAC insignia. Nowadays both building and airline are known by different names. A predatory line of taxis waits to pounce on customers from the Airways terminal or Victoria Coach Station which is opposite. Route 11 had a weekend allocation from Gillingham Street, Victoria garage and as was often the case this RTL is only going as far as Aldwych, not reaching the last named via point shown on the route blind. (D.F.Parker)

RT4490, complete with raised Green Line motif adorning its two tone green livery, is seen at Aldgate bus and coach station sometime during December. Route blinds are set for a journey to Grays by way of Route 723A on this RT whose appearance belies its six years of service. Although really just basic RTs, the lack of any commercial advertising always gave the Green Line versions the required air of superiority over their service bus counterparts. (A.R.Packer)

RF497 is seen at Stamford Hill operating a 'When Working' journey off the 236 from Stoke Newington to Tottenham Garage. Although correctly displaying the Tottenham destination it does not seem to have picked up many passengers on this busy stretch of road. It could be that people did not realise this little single decker could be used as an alternative to the trolleybuses and RTWs they might otherwise have caught and it is not likely the crew would have been keen to advise them of the fact. After twenty years service the bus found further use with the Normand Electrical Co.Ltd. of Cosham as a staff bus and although acquired for preservation it was scrapped in July 1987 having spent its last years as a store shed. (M.Dryhurst)

London Wall had been only recently widened and extended through to Aldersgate Street when, on a Saturday morning in July, RT2125 operated on a Railway Emergency Service. Buses replaced trains on the Circle and Metropolitan lines while massive construction projects were in hand and this traffic free length of roadway provides a perfect solution for the inconvenienced traveller. (M.Dryhurst)

The familiar outline of the 1912 built Palmers Green garage in Regents Avenue forms the background to this December picture of RT2764 in its final London guise, fitted with the body first carried by RT738. A lorry seems to be occupying the normal stand for 112 buses and the driver has emphasised this by leaving his bus at an awkward angle further up the road. The via point blind for this route was a little odd since the first line described pretty well all of the route while only specific places in the western half are mentioned. (A.R.Packer)

A comparison with the picture of RT176, which appears on page 32 of the 1954 book of this series, will clearly show the differences made to the front blind boxes. In the colour scheme of its new owners, Clyde Coast Services of Saltcoats, a load of school children are on board for the homeward journey including two who in typical fashion put their feet up on the front window ledge upstairs. The driver can be seen climbing into the cab before departure and the usual noisy journey will commence, although, compared to present day standards, at least this group seem to know that seats are for sitting in rather than standing on. (J.A.S.Hambley collection)

GS84 lays over in Crawley bus station displaying no route details or garage duty plates but fitted with a slipboard proclaiming 'EXTRA' in this sunny afternoon June view. In February Crawley had received an additional GS to provide an increased service on Route 434 largely by means of duplicates between Crawley and Crawley Down. This bus had been transferred from Leatherhead to Crawley during June and it may be assumed that it was this extra duty referred to on the board. (M.Dryhurst)

The North Terminal of Gatwick Airport now occupies most of the background of this picture making a present day comparison very difficult. An early morning in June witnesses RT4755 complete with unpainted wheel trims waiting for passengers while engaged on Works Service 853A with Faraday Road showing in the destination box and 'via North Road' as the only intermediate point. Garaged at Crawley since June 1958 its stay would last until entry into Works for its first overhaul during July 1962. (M.Dryhurst)

Former STL2694 now in the ownership of the Grimsby-Cleethorpes Joint Transport undertaking, which was formed on 1st January 1957, still carries the fleet number 44 allocated to the bus when initially acquired by Grimsby Corporation in August 1955 from the dealer, W.North. It is seen outside the bus garage in Victoria Street North on 28th May. The Weymann body still carries the distinctive flared lower panelling although the original one-piece front route box has been rebuilt while there is no sign of the one once carried above the platform. Serving the citizens of the two towns beside the Humber estuary until withdrawn in 1967, the bus appears more at ease than during its London operations when it looked completely alien to any London Transport inspired products. (J.C.Gillham)

RTL1300, looking smart in its green livery, approaches the New Town Centre at Hatfield along St. Albans Road on its way to St. Albans and Marshalswick. The mountings for the trafficators are in place but it is still necessary for the driver to signal his intention to turn right by hand. The side advertisement encourages commuting to town by Green Line, which in 1960 was still a viable alternative to the steam or diesel services offered by British Rail. (A.Mortimer)

Adverse weather conditions appear to have abated for a while allowing this view of RTL1555 with snow encrusted front end. The 18 series of routes have a long and convoluted history, too vast for a caption, but by 1960 the 18B variant had been reduced to being a weekday service operated by Middle Row garage between Harlesden, Willesden Junction where this bus is seen and London Bridge. In January 1962 it would be swept aside in the Harrow Road trolleybus conversion. (F.W.Ivey)

RTL1262 waits for its next trip on the 27th August from St. Mary's Square, Hitchin with conflicting route information. The via blind shows the display for the 303 route via Bell Bar while everything else indicates a 303A journey via Welham Green. Comment was made in the 1959 book of this series about advertisements for the Radio Show. The 1960 event at Earls Court features here showing the continued popularity of this medium. (A.R.Packer)

RT478 en-route for the Elephant & Castle on the 177 leads an RT operating on the 163 with a variety of other traffic at the busy New Cross Gate road junction. The subject RT had received its last overhaul in March 1958 being outshopped with bodywork of a type now earmarked for earliest disposal, which in this case was January 1964 to Bird's Commercial Motors of Stratford-upon-Avon. A very dainty Volkswagen Karmann-Ghia coupé glides past the bus while a Fordson Thames delivery van is half framed by the rear platform of the RT. (A.Mortimer)

This nearside view of RF10 serves to complement other offside pictures of the bus, which have appeared in earlier volumes of this series of books. It is parked at Victoria Station during April, having been returned to service after its final overhaul in January. Already it has sustained damage to the nearside bottom front corner panel and it is noticeable that a garage stencil plate is carried rather than displaying the painted identification now adopted by Central Area garages. The initial fittings for the eventual flashing trafficator can just be made out at the top of the front pillar to the saloon entrance. (A.R.Packer)

This line-up of former RTLs in the ownership of J.Laurie of Hamilton, Lanarkshire is not really what it first appears to be. From left to right the registrations indicate RTL1403, 336, 52 and 13. However, following the overhaul activities of Aldenham Works, the bodies are actually those originally carried by RTL5, 280, 74 and 70 and they are mounted on the original chassis of RTL1375, 307, 1434 and 1381. These combinations carried fleet numbers 45, 71, 68 and 53 with the 'Chieftain' fleet name until the business was taken over by Central SMT in October 1961. (A.J.Douglas)

RTWs garaged at Tottenham were the dominant allocation on Route 41 prior to the sixth stage of the trolleybus conversion programme. In the upper picture RTW104 with RTW320 parked closely behind wait on the stand outside the Hope & Anchor public house at Tottenham Hale on 21st April. A week later the route would be used to replace part of trolleybus 687, being withdrawn from its peak hour extension to Ilford and extended on weekdays instead to Stratford. RMs were introduced from West Ham garage and in the lower picture RM61 waits at Stratford Broadway on Saturday 12th November before a journey to Highgate, Archway Station. (Top - J.H.Aston; bottom - A.R.Packer)

London Road, Romford garage operated the summer only 726 Green Line Whipsnade Zoo route and in 1960 it was run in service from Romford Market with a return journey on Sunday coming from Harold Hill, Petersfield Avenue. RT3237 is seen one Saturday in June of the year under review negotiating the Hampstead Road/Tottenham Court Road junction at Warren Street Station which now bears no resemblance to its former layout. With a Ford Escort 100E car and the full skirts of the women's dresses the sixties era appears to be getting into full swing. (M.Dryhurst)

Extremes of seating capacity are shown in this picture of 56 seat RTL1265 and the dinky three wheeler Messerschmitt behind. Halfway through receiving trafficators the bus carries a slipboard which reads 'To and From Hitchin Market' that is probably aimed more at the residents of Stevenage rather than Hatfield, which is where in Cavendish Way this picture is taken as the driver turns into the part of St. Albans Road which is now a dead end but which in 1960 led to the Stonehouse. Many of the passengers of this well loaded vehicle appear to be attracted to the activities of the photographer. After much controversy all eighteen of these green liveried RTLs would be taken out of service less that a year after their introduction due chiefly to the dislike of them by the Country Area drivers. (A.Mortimer)

RT729 had initially entered passenger service in July 1948 garaged at Catford followed by later use at Abbey Wood before its arrival at Hendon following an overhaul in December 1959. Heading south along King William Street on Route 13, the driver has already wound the destination blind for the return journey from London Bridge Station which lies just across the river. (D.F.Parker)

Green Line liveried RF305 works a pre-Green Line duty on bus route 396 to Bishops Stortford with its 720 boards already in place on a rather wet morning. The registration identity was carried by Country Area bus RF524 until, together with several others it was converted to Green Line configuration and renumbered during the spring of 1956. (A.Mortimer)

RM177 departs Walthamstow garage on 12th March to take up duties from the Crooked Billet terminal of Route 58 to Canning Town which had been re-introduced on 3rd February to replace trolleybus 685. The new number, which bore some relationship, had been vacant since the Golders Green to Archway service had been withdrawn in August 1958. Before the year ended this bus had been delicensed and was then used for learner duties until it settled down in regular passenger service once again at Shepherds Bush in June 1964. (R.B.Partridge)

RM176 on Route 58 the replacement for the 685 trolleybus lacks a stencil or painted indication as to its home base of Walthamstow. The total lack of television aerials on the terraced housing of Crownfield Road is notable and various contemporary vans and a motorcycle and sidecar combination add to a scene now long passed. (M.Dryhurst)

Reference to page 121 of the 1954 volume of this series will reveal another body which carried the fleet number RT1903. With the emergence of the bus from overhaul at Aldenham Works in July 1958 Saunders body number 7350 was fitted. Service at no fewer than nine different garages then ensued before the bus settled down at Hounslow during December 1959 and so remained until its next overhaul in July 1962. It waits in the yard of Twickenham Station prior to departure back to Hounslow garage. (John A.S.Hambley collection)

Introduced on 26th January 1957, Route 263 operated on Saturdays only between the now closed Coulsdon North Station and Clock House Farm Estate, which backed on to the Woodcote Park Golf Course. It was worked by a lone Croydon RT and ran between 10a.m. and 5 p.m. with an hour's break for lunch. The hilly nature of the short route is perhaps reflected by its eight minute outward journey time and seven minutes return. In 1964 the route passed out of London Transport's hands to Banstead Coaches. On 19th November RT4582 is seen at the Coulsdon North terminal with a good number of people eager to be carried up the hill. (A.R.Packer)

Abridge situated in the Essex countryside beyond Epping Forest was the furthest point reached by a Route 10 bus in 1960 which had as its central London termini Victoria or London Bridge station according to the day of the week. At its countryside terminal, identified by the unusual bus stop mounted directly on the brickwork of the adjacent 'Blue Boar' public house, Gillingham Street's RTL813 waits departure on its hour and half journey back to Victoria. (A.Mortimer)

The two pictures on this page illustrate the joint working in 1960 of Route 238 which ran from Becontree to Canning Town with a peak hour extension to North Woolwich. Both RMs are at the top of Silvertown Way, Canning Town heading back to their respective garages. In the upper picture RM27 is about to turn right and aim for West Ham Garage, which was more or less on line of route, while below RM128, one of Poplar's contribution, turns left destined for Poplar, Aberfeldy Street which was off route. Although the trolleybus wires have been removed the traction poles have been retained since they served the dual purpose of street lampposts. (Both A.B.Cross)

RW2 is seen in service on a sunny autumn Sunday at Hemel Hempstead, Warners End on Route 322A. In the top picture the driver can be seen attending to a passenger with hand outstretched awaiting his change. The bottom picture shows the treatment of the rear offside to accommodate the emergency exit. The route number box would appear to have been an LT requirement on the more or less standard Willowbrook body. (A.Mortimer)

The route number 70 had lain unused as far as buses were concerned from 14th January 1942 until reincarnation with stage four of the tram to bus conversion programme on 11th July 1951 when it replaced the tram route of the same number. Initially it operated from Greenwich to London Bridge extended weekdays to Waterloo but by 1960 the extreme termini had been expanded to Eltham and Victoria. On 12th October of the year under review it would be cut back again from Eltham to Greenwich but prior to that on 2nd July New Cross garaged RT2986 waits at Waterloo before leaving on the 05.34 departure. (A.R.Packer)

Despite the fact that in June when this photograph was taken none of the trolleybus routes which served the Nags Head junction at Holloway had been withdrawn, you could be forgiven for thinking the reverse, bearing in mind that buses dominate this scene. Careful inspection though does reveal an L3 class trolleybus following the two kerbside vehicles. RTW472 operating on Route 14 to Hornsey Rise and RTL173 in service on the 172 demonstrate well how just six inches additional width of the former makes the 7'6" wide RTL look somewhat insubstantial. (M.Dryhurst)

Having changed its allegiance from Central Area duties to that of the Country Area with a change of colour less than three years after its initial entry into service, RT4438 is now garaged at Hatfield. It is seen in Welwyn Garden City bus station soon to depart on the convoluted town service 324 with advertising for the well-publicised Pamphilon fabric shop situated in St. Albans. (A.Mortimer)

Having emerged from beneath the Underground railway bridge in Turnham Green Terrace, Southall garaged RT329 on Route 55 continues its journey to Chiswick Station. This terminus was used when for various reasons buses scheduled to terminate at the Grove Park Hotel could not access the Grove Park bridge over the railway. In later years the Grove Park terminal was described as 'Chiswick Station, Grove Park Hotel' adding confusion. Last overhauled in October 1958, the bus would continue in passenger service until April 1963 followed by periods in use as a staff bus or trainer garaged at Tring. Finally delicensed in July 1970 it was sold in February 1971 to preservationist Tony Sheldon. (J.A.S.Hambley collection)

Stage 6 of the trolleybus conversion programme on 27th April made use of the vacant route number 123 with the introduction of a service between Manor House Station and Ilford Station replacing practically all of the erstwhile trolleybus route 623 and the peak hour extension of Route 41 to Ilford. The new service however ran daily through to Ilford. Walthamstow garage provided the larger number of buses for the service as typified by RM213 in the upper picture seen in Seven Sisters Road heading for the Manor House terminal. On Mondays to Saturdays Tottenham garage provided some RTWs and in the lower picture RTW136, by this time actually using the chassis and body of the original RTW154, waits at Manor House during December before a short journey to Beacontree Avenue at Walthamstow. The L.T. Divisional Offices and Medical Centre in the old tramway offices can be seen to the right of the picture. (Both A.R.Packer)

On 19th June the photographer witnessed T790 arriving at Two Waters from Tring garage with no garage or duty plates in place but showing '707 OXTED' on the blind as depicted in the upper picture. After a crew change and the addition of running plates, the blinds were rewound and it departed for London as a 706 Green Line Relief as seen in the lower picture. During their operational career with London Transport stretching from 1948 through to 1962 various Country Area garages used 15T13s at times as Green Line reliefs but it was not all that common an occurrence.
(Both P.J.Malsher)

Unusually transferred in August to the then RTL and RM stocked Shepherds Bush garage RT1184 soon found itself on an unusual route, the 268, which was the preserve of the RM class vehicles. Caught by the camera at Butterwick, Hammersmith, the Saunders bodied RT was transferred to the more compatible Walworth garage the following month. The passenger shelter indicates that the stop is served by routes 11, 220, 268, night bus 297 and trolleybus 655. On October 12th night route 297 would be renumbered N97, while early in November trolleybus 655 would be replaced by bus 255. (W.R.Legg)

Green liveried RLH2 is seen arriving at Clapton Pond on Route 178 during its only period of loan to the Central Area at Dalston garage during September and October of the year under review. Since its last overhaul in December 1956 it had been garaged at Addlestone and would return there after its brief excursion into east London. Behind a class M1 trolleybus, number 1538 continues its journey on service 653 to Finsbury Park Station. (F.W.Ivey)

Former RTL4 was one of eight of the class purchased by O.K.Motor Services of Bishops Auckland in March 1958. Seen at the railway station in its new home town, the bus wears the maroon, red and cream livery of this respected operator who had started running a bus service on a regular basis on Easter Monday 1912. Although the registration mark indicates RTL4, the body is actually that carried by the original RTL3, while the chassis is that of RTL1344. This combination came together at Aldenham Works as RTL4 after overhaul in January 1956. A photograph of the vehicle prior to this change can be found in the 1955 supplement to this volume. During January 1969 the bus would be dismantled to provide spares for other RTLs still owned. (C.S.Marshall)

The forecourt of the Royal Forest Hotel provided the terminal for many routes over the years until the requirements of the car owning customers ousted them from this picturesque watering hole in 1968. In this July view are, from left to right, RM217, RTW264, RM177, RT2017 and RT2010. They are serving three routes, the older vehicles on the very long standing 38 and 102 while the Routemasters are on the new 257 which had first arrived on the forecourt on 3rd February, being an extended replacement for trolleybus 557. (A.B.Cross)

Former RT1496 in the upper picture has had its roof number box removed with the roof dome now requiring a coat of paint to complete the alteration, while in the lower picture ex-RT1478 demonstrates the completed job including new operator's fleetname below the lower saloon windows. Both vehicles are owned by T. Hunter of Kilmarnock, part of the A1 Services Ltd. consortium. In the background of the lower picture ex-RT1436, operated by another member, Kerr & Linney, was to retain its roof box throughout its years of operation. As can be seen, this owner member adopted a slightly different paint scheme. Ardrossan is the location of both views. (D.F.Parker)

Standing outside the Park Royal factory RM489 together with RM498 wait for delivery to Aldenham works sometime during September. The lead bus is fully decked out with advertising material contrasting sharply with the uncluttered bodywork of the vehicle behind. Both classified 6/5RM5/6 they are representative of the largest externally identical batch of 570 RM bodies delivered during the period May 1960 to September 1961. In tandem after a short period stored at Mortlake garage these two buses entered passenger service from Hanwell garage as part of the large number required for new routes 207, 207A and 255 which replaced trolleybus services 607 and 655 on 9th November. (Photobus)

The railway replacement service in connection with the Central Line extension over the former LNER steam lines finally ran in November 1948. It used open staircase LTs, specially made route blinds and the bus stops were of a permanent nature. At the last stage only a service to cover the Hainault to Woodford section was required although because of the road topography of the area buses served Woodford before running on to Roding Valley. In Madeira Grove, Woodford LT20 faces the camera en-route for Hainault while LT46 is soon to depart in the opposite direction to Roding Valley. LT46 was to be withdrawn from service before the end of the year while the other bus lasted a little longer until scrapped in the following June. (Omnibus Society)

The terminal stand within the roundabout at Muswell Hill Broadway must be among, if not the, longest serving suburban bus stand in London. Photographs exist of horse buses standing in this very spot. On 30th October 1948 un-renovated LT1030 with blinds reset for a journey to the Capitol Cinemas at Winchmore Hill by way of Route 244 is kept company by four months old RT695 before it departs to Victoria on Route 134. (A.B.Cross)

With running plates WG2, LT1145 stands with STLs, LTs and a lone RT in this view taken at Victoria Station. This bus must be considered a very temporary loan from Muswell Hill garage as no mention is made of the vehicle in the very detailed history of West Green garage which has appeared in the Bulletins of the London Historical Research Group of the Omnibus Society. Note the body sag immediately below the obvious roof repair, no doubt one of the contributory factors leading to its withdrawal in March 1950, the body being scrapped and the chassis stripped of all useful parts. (L.T.P.S.)

Q214 has appeared in the 1957 book of this series after its disposal but in happier times it stands outside its home garage of Hertford dressed for use on a route which had been associated with the class since 1936. Pre-war versions of the 715 operated as routes M1, M2 and M3 but these, in line with all other Green Line routes ceased operation during the Second World War. From September 1939 to December 1945 this vehicles served as a public ambulance before returning to pick up its pre-war occupation at Hertford. (D.A.Thompson)

In 1949 it was always exciting to pay a visit to the conveniently placed Park Royal works in west London to see the latest vehicles awaiting delivery. RT1536 gleams in the August sunshine lacking only licensing and a set of route blinds before entry into service at Dalston garage is achieved. (R.A.Golds)

During its last few weeks in service LT1003 has made a journey to the big city substituting for a double deck LT or RT carrying running plates T42. It had been transferred to Leyton garage during January 1948 for use on their Route 236 allocation but SRT69 in the background working from Cricklewood on the 16 route narrows down the date on which this scene could have occurred prior to the single deck's disposal during October 1949 to Daniels of Rainham for scrap. (J.A.S.Hambley collection)

The blown rubbish in the background suggests a windy day at Epsom Downs. Tree lopper 650J holds up following traffic while the driver in conversation with an inspector resolves some sort of problem. Presumably not on lopping duties it may be on its way to serve as a grandstand for some private party to the races. New in July 1930 to Thomas Tilling Ltd. as a 52 seat open staircase bus, it carried fleet number 6041 until given the identity of ST865 in 1933 by LPTB. It was withdrawn from service in October 1944 for conversion to its new role. Finally disposed of to Moore and Porter, a dealer of Mitcham in November 1953 it must be presumed that it was eventually scrapped. (I.Pearce)

On Whit Monday, 6th June, red STL2093 acts as a relief on Green Line Route 703 with running numbers SJ103 and is about to depart from Eccleston Bridge, Victoria for Wrotham. Originally fitted with Park Royal all-metal bodywork, this had been replaced with the LPTB built composite example seen here two months previous. This had been retrieved from the chassis of STL2570 when that went for SRT conversion. Receiving an overhaul in January 1951 the bus continued in this form until withdrawn in February 1954. It then spent one year as a learner vehicle before disposal to W. North, the dealer of Leeds, occurred in June 1955. (A.B.Cross)

The registration plate and both the brass dumb iron plates fitted by London Transport confirm the origins of this AEC Regal with Strachan 32 seat bodywork. Starting life in 1930 as an LGOC bodied 27 seat Green Line coach, fleet number T105, its ownership by the Board ended in December 1938. Disposed of to the Arlington Motor Company, the London dealer, it was subsequently acquired by Valliant Coaches of Ealing in May 1939. They had the new bodywork fitted and eventually it was sold on to Manns Way Coaches of Beaconsfield in April 1949, in whose livery it is seen at an Epsom race meeting. (J.A.S.Hambley collection)

In bright sunshine passengers board Hendon's STD95 for the homeward journey to the tube at Morden after a day at the racing on Epsom Downs. Two policemen provide rather languid crowd control while the school capped boy clutches a notebook which is more likely to contain bus numbers than racing form. On the left a fine array of coaches wait to transport further punters home from their day out and the conviviality of the journey may well depend on their success at the bookies. (I.Pearce)

An inspector and the well-dressed conductress converse with the driver of LT1031 in this view taken at Bromley-by-Bow. Marshalls of Cambridge had carried out renovation and repaint of the LGOC built bodywork during the early months of 1949. Currently powered by a petrol engine, this would be replaced by a diesel unit in June of the following year. Transferred then to Kingston garage it would soldier on in its new guise as a 1LTL1/2 until withdrawal in January 1953. (D.A.Jones)

For a few years after the Second World War the Derby race meeting at Epsom provided enthusiasts with what was often the last chance to see aged vehicles in service before they were scrapped. ST513 with the 'Tobler' advertisement is a case in point. Here at the beginning of June it has been sent to the races by Cricklewood garage. It would be withdrawn on the 16th and by the end of the month would be in Daniels' Rainham scrapyard. ST485 behind would actually see in January 1950 before it too would find itself in Daniels' yard. The circular signs on the left of the photograph carry the words 'Bonnet Stop' to help drivers position their buses at the loading bays at the end of the day. The term 'Headstop' had obviously not yet come into use. (R.A.Golds)

STL420 started life in May 1934 garaged at Chalk Farm, which by October of that year was surpassed only by Willesden in the number of the class then allocated to the garage. The last nine years of service were spent in the Country Area, having been repainted green in July 1944. Standing in the St. Albans garage forecourt it waits departure for a journey to Harperbury Hospital by way of Route 338. After disposal in 1954, the Eagre Construction Company of Scunthorpe would make use of the vehicle for approximately three years. (J.A.S.Hambley collection)

Since January 1950 ST1059 had been in use as a learner bus garaged at Reigate. Re-enacting its previous past, it is seen at Tattenham Corner on a one-day private hire outing sometime during the June race meeting. Immediately returning to learner duties until the end of the year it was then disposed of to Daniels of Rainham who reduced to scrap a bus whose history started with the East Surrey Traction Company in June 1931. (R.A.Golds)

The Grays garage building stands to the left of this picture which shows TF29 neatly parked after its previous journey from Aldgate on Route 723. The ubiquitous watering can for topping up radiators sits perched on the corner flagstone. Seventy-five of these handsome LPTB bodied coaches entered service in 1939 and at the end of passenger use the vast majority were disposed of in 1953. The exceptions being five dismantled at Chiswick Works during 1952 and the one example, TF77, donated to the London Transport Collection in 1954. (R.A.Golds)

— 1951 —

During its last months of operation STL1889 is seen en-route for Crystal Palace on Route 2 carrying a healthy load of passengers in Brixton. Conduited tram track with block paving occupies the central part of the thoroughfare but by the summer of the following year a smooth tarmac finish would cover the whole width of the roadway. Of note is the modern London Transport tram stop flag with its blue roundel looking totally out of place on the venerable L.C.C. stop post. The bus was withdrawn from service in June 1951 but continued as a learner vehicle through to December 1953 whereupon it was disposed of to W.North in the following month. (F.W.Ivey)

RTL668 operated from Edgware garage through most of 1951 before further transfer to Barking in the final month of the year. With running number EW4 it is seen en-route for Mill Hill on Route 140 on a decidedly quiet day. Originally entering service in February 1950 at Riverside its ownership with London Transport would end in November 1966 when disposed of for further service in South Africa. (R.Wellings)

Still wearing its Green Line livery but with a London Transport fleetname, D165 stands at the Hampton Court Station terminus of Route 152. Originally entering service in March 1946 as part of the programme to re-open the heavily trafficked East End Green Line routes running out of Aldgate, the Daimlers were replaced by new RTs commencing in late 1950. Transferred to Merton garage all would receive Central Area livery during 1951 making them indistinguishable from most of the other members of the class at that south-west London garage. (D.F.Parker)

One person operated C22 with Northfleet garage plate but no running number and sparse route information waits on the Route 489 stand in the depressing surroundings of inner Gravesend before setting out on a journey to Longfield. This bus ended its British service at Northfleet in December 1953, ousted by GSs, but was not disposed of until September 1954. It then went via W.North Ltd. of Leeds to the South Western Omnibus Company (Ceylon) where it was lengthened to accommodate 41 passengers and re-registered IC2438 surviving until the end of the decade. (D.F.Parker)

The driver of TF65 prepares to indicate to the following traffic his intentions to pull out from the bus stop in St. Peters Street, St. Albans on 23rd October to continue his shortened journey to Radlett by way of Route 355. Downgraded to bus work and now wearing 'London Transport' fleet name, it was to last exactly one year in its new role before being disposed of to W.North. The Leeds dealer was involved in handling seventy-one of the class of eighty-eight vehicles. (J.C.Gillham)

TF17 is seen departing from New Barnet Station on a journey to Broxbourne Station on Route 342 wearing Green Line fleetnames with running number HG32. 1952 was one of the eventful years for the TF class since with the exception of just three examples they were all downgraded from Green Line duties to Country Area bus work with the influx of the new RF class. By the July of the following year all had been disposed of except for TF77 which continues in the care of London's Transport Museum. (L.C.C.Tramways Trust)

Commencing in September 1951 48 RTs were painted with a revised experimental livery and RT1152 displays its all-red finish only relieved by the between decks cream band. The revised colour scheme was applied to the buses as they passed through their normal overhaul, with the wheels, mudguards and lifeguards all finished in red. After their initial use on Route 2 from Cricklewood and Norwood garages they were quickly dispersed around the system, this example returning to its original home when new of Muswell Hill. It is outside the soon to be demolished Grand Hall at North Finchley when photographed on Route 125 on 14th August. (J.A.S.Hambley collection)

The small orderly and patient queue formed at a bus stop in Halliford Road give the impression that it is not LT1080 on its Route 237 journey to Chertsey Station that they require. Maybe a 264 to Walton is what is needed. There does however seem to be some interest being displayed in the area of the nearside front wheel. The bus, although one of those that escaped the refurbishment programme by Marshalls of Cambridge, had been fitted with a diesel engine in May 1950 and was to soldier on almost to the demise of the class in January 1953. (D.F.Parker)

— 1953 —

Waiting in the vicinity of Morden Station for its call into service on the Epsom Race Course special service, STL935 looks rather austere with its painted radiator shell and wheel trims in this June photograph. In store for over a year along with many others of the type, it was brought back into service in the Coronation year and would eventually be one of the last red liveried members of the class to be disposed of. (R.A.Golds)

Epsom railway station and the Route 406F special race meeting buses look uncannily quiet with London Transport employees outnumbering the public by five to one. Centre piece RT3487 has come from Staines for the day, while in the background newly overhauled RT1449 had only recently re-entered service at Streatham. The signal box and petrol pump capture the flavour of the period very well. (R.A.Golds)

In May 1953 this fairly short lived version of Route 243 was withdrawn and Enfield's TD46 transferred to Kingston garage together with the remaining examples of the class that had worked their since new. Standing beneath the trolleybus wiring at Waltham Cross it waits for a new crew to continue its journey to Flamstead End at Cheshunt. The route number had previously been used for the Peckham-Nunhead circular service and would now remain conveniently unused until needed to replace the Wood Green to Holborn Circus trolleybus routes 543/643. (D.F.Parker)

Ex-T10 together with a single deck LT, which just could be LT1040 (GO656), and a pair of former provincial buses are all in use as caravans behind the New Castle Inn at Colchester sometime during November 1953. It was reported that the T class bus had departed this grassy environment by 1956 although no reports appear to have been recorded with regard to the LT. Both London Transport vehicles had originally been sold to Daniels of Rainham in October 1949. (R.A.Golds)

T532 works out its last few months of passenger service at Central Area Kingston garage in green livery. It is seen at the Staines West Station terminal of Route 218 fitted with the standard 1940s style of single deck route blind which gave an immense amount of detail. (D.F.Parker)

Weymann bodied Leyland Cub C93 initially entered service in May 1936 as one of twenty-two small capacity buses for lightly trafficked Central Area routes. One of the most notable differences between this batch and their Short bodied sisters was the lack of a front bumper. Repainted in Country Area colours in May 1950 and thereafter garaged at Northfleet, this example continued in service until withdrawn in January 1954. It and the now preserved C94, were the last operational pair at this garage and the last of the Weymann bodied members of the class. In surroundings typical of those served by the Cubs the bus is en-route for Singlewell on Route 490 in its last full year of operation.

(J.A.S.Hambley collection)

Front entrance Weymann bodied STL1488 was disposed of during July 1951 and was eventually acquired by the London Institute of Education in 1952. Here in the following year work progresses on transforming it into an open top vehicle with enclosed lower saloon. In addition a door was fitted to the driver's cab. The reason for the conversion is unclear as in February 1954 it was acquired by Costain the building contractors. (G.E.Baddeley)

Hitchin garage had the honour of placing the first of the new GS class into service in the northern Country Area during October, replacing an elderly C type on Route 383. GS2 is about to depart St. Mary's Square, Hitchin on one of the short eight minute journeys to the Purwell Lane Estate at Walsworth. In the background of this November scene C31 is prepared for a short working of Route 386 to Great Wymondley in this its final month of revenue earning duties before being sold to W.North Ltd. the dealer of Leeds. (R.A.Golds)

In June STL542 departs from Epsom Downs on the Special Service to Morden. The paper sticker on the blind has come unstuck but the full load of punters know where they are going. It carries CL1 as a running number and would continue in service from Clayhall until the end of the month when it was delicensed to await disposal. Originally entering service in August 1934 as a 7STL3/2 it ended its career as a 2/16STL18 having been converted from petrol to diesel. (R.A.Golds)

Having initially entered service in November 1953, Dunton Green's GS27 waits at Orpington Station before departure on the circular route 471. It is working in the direction requiring the blind display with the intriguing and somewhat comical top line 'PRATTS BOTTOM (CIRCULAR)'. The route was exclusively operated by these 26 seat buses until the last day of 1966 when one-man operated RFs took over the duties. Two years previous to that this GS had departed company with London Transport and following a chequered career was broken up by outside contractors on the premises of Hendon Car Sales, London NW2 in December 1968. One wonders whether it had been part exchanged for a saloon car. (J.A.S Hambley collection)

SRT155 first entered service in January 1950 from Harrow Weald garage primarily for use on Route 114. Transferred to Chalk Farm for Route 196 in August of the same year, this was followed by a move to Barking for Route 66A in October 1952. Finally transferred to North Street, Romford upon the opening of the new garage there in August 1953, it continued in service until withdrawal in August of the following year. The bus never received an overhaul but the body was later used to form RT4525. (R.A.Golds)

There seems to be some confusion in this April scene as GS66 and a 10T10 have both arrived at the 394 stop in Chesham. The GS driver has his passenger door firmly closed and seems undecided as to whether he is going to go to Chartridge or beat a hasty retreat to Amersham garage. The driver of the T, who appears to be displaying a choice of Great Missenden or Lee Common, has climbed from his cab looking determined to sort out the GS driver. Meanwhile the bemused passengers can only stand and wait. So much for the alleged 'good old days'! (R.A.Golds)

Plumstead garaged RTL440 is working the special excursion service between Bexleyheath and Charlton Football Ground in March 1954. At this time the 'Addicks' were still a First Division side and the Leyland PS coach of Southdown Motor Services has doubtless brought supporters from further afield for the match at The Valley. The RTL is one of those equipped with semaphore arm trafficators as shown by the vertical black stripe beneath the empty running plate holder which is the offside unit. (R.A.Golds)

RT42 still looks immaculate after fourteen years' passenger service, the first five of which involved keeping out of the way of enemy activity. Roughly just twelve months remain of passenger use although it had only received its final Chiswick overhaul during October 1953. It retains its polished wheel trims and restricted front blind display although this is now in the process of being converted to full use again. The bus stands at Southfields on the special service to the Wimbledon Tennis Championships. One wonders whether the Evening Standard advertisement would be accepted nowadays. (R.A.Golds)

Route 238 operating between Noak Hill and Emerson Park was one of the more obscure Central Area routes and was one man operated until July 1949. Ts replaced Cs and subsequently new TDs took over operation from the Ts. During April 1954 the route was double decked and one RT replaced the three TDs scheduled on the route. Before this change TD84 is seen at Parkstone Avenue in the final month of single deck working. It is standing alongside a tree suffering from the recent somewhat severe pruning efforts of the local authority parks department. (R.A.Golds)

1955

The large expanse of space at the Fulwell Depot has been put to good use on a number of occasions for the storage of vehicles awaiting disposal. The Q1 trolleybus 1804 parked at the site entrance has a number years service left unlike the line-up of STLs. STL930, 868, 698, 1792, 537 and 1915 were all despatched to W.North of Leeds during the following months but before they depart it is interesting to note that STL698 still carries a pre-1950 livery while 1792 and 1915 wear Country Area colours. (N.Rayfield)

The low angle at which this picture was taken allows a good view of the canopy route number box, illuminated both day and night when first introduced. This feature, operated by a small outside handle reached by sitting on the top of the nearside wing, was incorporated on all RT family bodies built without the roof box number blind. RTL4 is seen with the decaying Crystal Palace High Level station in the background which had been closed the previous year. (D.F.Parker)

Ample light penetrates the interior of New Cross garage to reveal RT21 with sister RT64 parked to its right still carrying a full set of blinds. The chassis of SRT138, in use as a slave for a brand new RT body, is backed up against the wall behind. Central Area passenger operation of the 'pre-war' RT class had ceased on the last day of May 1955. These two buses now had a few years use as staff buses or trainers to look forward to before their disposal. RT64 would find its way to Bird's for scrap in December 1960 but RT21 went via Lammas Motors of Battersea in 1963 to Mountnessing Autospares in Essex. They in turn sold it to the Aztecs Beat Group in January 1964 so it presumably had a noisy end to its life. (D.F.Parker)

The supplement for the year 1956 contained in the 1957 book of this series includes a picture of several Craven bodied RTs destined for operation with Dundee Corporation. As a comparison this view is included showing four of the total of ten 18STL20s acquired twelve months earlier and parked within the same BRS yard at Dock Street, Dundee in August. The LT bonnet numbers from left to right are STL2698, 2684, 2687 and 2685 with the first still fitted with a Garston garage blind as a reminder of its previous operating base. All four later entered service in Scotland's fourth largest city carrying fleet numbers 178, 170, 172 and 171 respectively. They were withdrawn en-bloc in December 1964 having given almost equal service to their two owners. (A.R.Packer)

Merton garaged RF371 is seen at the 'Prince's Head', Battersea before setting off, crew operated on Excursion 88 to Newlands Corner the well known beauty spot on the North Downs above Albury. The bus stop has a special sticker over the roundel for Sunday Bus Excursions. Excursion 88 was unusual in being single deck operated. (D.A.Jones)

Still basically in original condition, ex-B14 completed almost three years operation with Hartlepool Corporation carrying fleet number H3 before disposal in April 1956. The bus waits in Church Street, Hartlepool, close to the sea front and docks before a further journey. It is operated and staffed by Bee Line Roadways (Tees-Side) Ltd. of West Hartlepool, the crew being seconded to Corporation employment. (D.F.Parker)

— 1956 —

RT25 can be seen in the 1939-45 book of this series at the beginning of its career with London Transport. Here it is nearing the end of its life on 18th July 1956 in the service of Beeline Roadways of West Hartlepool, County Durham wearing that operator's blue and white livery. Beeline owned a number of double deckers and added RT25, 125 and 149 to its fleet in May 1956. All were put up for sale however in 1958 and RT25 found further work, mostly on contract duties, with S.& H.M.Connell trading as 'Ubique Coaches' of Maida Vale from May 1958 through to November 1963. (A.R.Packer)

Transferred to Kingston garage on 8th August, Country Area T794 attracts a healthy number of passengers at the town's railway station before departure on Route 216 to Staines via Ashford. The rest of the vehicle's service in London would be in this south-west corner of the capital, albeit later garaged at Norbiton but always wearing the Coutnry Area green. On 20th January 1959 it would represent, together with T773, 784 and 786, the very last use of the single deck T class in passenger service on Central Area routes. (J.H.Aston)

Between August 1954 and early 1962 former C57 was owned by the Mansfield House Settlement organisation of Fairborn Hall, London E3 in a non-p.s.v. capacity. In remarkably unaltered condition it is seen here in Stockwell in May 1957. It was sighted in 1962 on the premises of T.Watkinson, a dealer of Ripple Road, Barking but enquiries have not revealed any further information with regard to its ultimate fate. (J.A.S.Hambley collection)

Ex-STL1700 is parked somewhere in Hackney during March minus its engine. Was it removed by thieves while the driver enjoyed a 'fry-up' in the adjacent café ? For a period following sale by the Executive in February 1954 it had been owned by M.Charlton & Sons Ltd. of Fourstones, a village to the west of Newcastle-upon-Tyne. Then sometime in 1956 it passed to Advance Precision Instruments Ltd. of Hainault, Essex, a fact confirmed by the name displayed in the destination box. It was withdrawn in December 1957 and sold to Walker Brothers, a dealer in Hackney. Presumably it has been towed here ready for scrap and the dealer's premises are in the vicinity. (B.Pask)

RT958 waits departure from Parsons Hill, Woolwich on a Route 161A journey to Chislehurst War Memorial on 13th September 1958. In the background beyond the trees Bexleyheath's trolleybuses are in their last year of operation. Having been transferred from Mortlake to Plumstead garage in March 1955 this RT was overhauled in December 1956 and continued at the south-east London location until November 1958. (R.A.Golds)

The 176A route originated as the replacement for tram service 60 and terminated in the City of London at Cannon Street. Dowgate Hill has a rather derelict air about it in this view taken on 9th August 1958. RTL913 is working the route from Walworth garage, the former Camberwell tram depot which also supplied the trackbound vehicles for the service. (R.A.Golds)

Route 56 followed a u-shaped course around the perimeter of the Isle of Dogs from Poplar in the east to Limehouse which was a mile away to the west as the crow flies. Apart from the present day double-run round Canary Wharf, this route is followed now by the D7 but in very different surroundings to those depicted here. A docked cargo ship towers above RTL1051 as it bounces over the cobbles on its way round to Limehouse. Overhauled in July 1958, the RTL was allocated to Athol Street garage where it remained until 10th May 1961 when it moved to nearby Poplar upon the closure of the Athol Street premises. (D.F.Parker)

Horse Guards Avenue, Westminster provides the elegant tree shrouded terminal for a number of routes including the short-lived 50A which commenced operation in October 1957 only to be withdrawn in August 1958. Double-parked RTL981 carries CA16 running numbers on 9th August, ten days before the route was withdrawn. Later in the year Clapham garage would cease operation and commence conversion to become the British Transport Museum. (R.A.Golds)

Pausing alongside the General Post Office in St. Martin-le-Grand RT2689 en-route for Finsbury Park Station on Route 4 is working from Old Kent Road garage on 9th August 1958. Ten days later this garage would cease its involvement with this route and three months later it would finally close. This version of Route 4 from Surrey Docks Station to Finsbury Park would survive until the end of 1966. (R.A.Golds)

RTW278 waits alongside one of its six-inch slimmer RTL counterparts in the Waterloo parking area on 1st August 1958. The extra width on the RTW is shown by the neater display of the front advertisements. The rubber mounted glazing to the blind boxes and thinner cream band between decks also distinguish the class from its contemporaries. The RTW is working a journey back to its home base at Hackney, Well Street on Route 6A. (R.A.Golds)

Standing outside its home garage of Chelsham on 26th October 1958, RT2512 displays the destination Farleigh, the nearby easterly terminal of Route 403B. Together with the main 403 service which then operated from Tonbridge and 403A variant serving Warlingham Park Hospital, the inter-worked routes journeyed through Croydon to Wallington. Few would have imagined in 1958 that one day in the future this would be a red bus route. (R.A.Golds)

RTW500, the highest numbered of the class, works a journey on 1958 Route 39A, which lasted from January through to November. It sought to provide a service on Sundays for visitors to St. Thomas' Hospital. The bus is crossing from Grosvenor Gardens into Victoria Street at the junction with Buckingham Palace Road on 2nd August. (R.A.Golds)

On 25th October 1958 RTL961 shows the high standard of finish to buses emerging from overhaul. Now garaged at Clapham it waits at the Wimbledon terminus of Route 155 before departing to Westminster and Embankment. In a month's time this route will be chiefly worked by Merton's RTs with a few RTLs from Stockwell on Saturdays after the closure of Clapham garage. (R.A.Golds)

The route number 51A was used to differentiate the service running to the Rose and Crown at Green Street Green rather than the main route which served Farnborough and at times continued to Bromley Garage in order to serve the hospital complex at Locks Bottom. On 13th September 1958 Sidcup garaged RT2882 with a stablemate parked closely behind wait their departure times to journey to one of the extremities of red bus operation. The Vespa scooter parked to the right was a very fashionable means of transport at this time. (R.A.Golds)

Standing at the Old Ford terminus on 18th October 1958 beside an ornate lamppost which probably started life fed by gas, Clayhall's RTW215 waits departure on a curtailed Route 8 journey to Kilburn, Quex Road. Behind, RTW207 will work through to Willesden Garage. (R.A.Golds)

— 1959 —

For a period of five years the former STL1511 with the lower saloon seating increased by six was used in service with R.Whieldon & Sons of Castle Donington. The draughts associated with this front entrance type of bodywork have been eliminated now that the boarding area has been rebuilt to include a door. Seen in the operator's home town during its last summer of operation, it was disposed of to Fleet Car Sales, a dealer of Dunchurch, in March 1960. (Mike A. Sutcliffe)

In the ownership of Rubery Owen & Co.Ltd. of Darlaston, Staffordshire, ex-C42 was used for engine development tests at their premises at Bourne in Lincolnshire for many years. It is seen in July 1959 with little external alteration although now fitted with an impressive array of headlamps and possibly some sort of demister to the upper portion of the windscreen. In 1960 it was despatched to J.Foster, a dealer in Bourne for scrap, thus ending a career which had commenced in June 1935. (Mike A.Sutcliffe)

APPENDIX I

London Transport Central and Country Area Bus Garages

A	Sutton	K	Kingston
AB	Twickenham	L	Loughton
AC	Willesden	LH*	Leatherhead
AD	Palmers Green	LS*	Luton
AE	Hendon	M	Mortlake
AF	Chelverton Road, Putney	MA*	Amersham
AK	Streatham	MH	Muswell Hill
AL	Merton	N	Norwood
AM	Plumstead	NB	Norbiton
AP	Seven Kings	NF*	Northfleet
AR	Tottenham	NS	North Street, Romford
AV	Hounslow	NX	New Cross
AW	Abbey Wood	ON	Alperton
B	Battersea	PB	Potters Bar
BK	Barking	PM	Peckham
BN	Brixton	PR	Poplar
BW	Bow	Q	Camberwell
BX	Bexleyheath	R	Riverside
C	Athol Street, Poplar	RD	Hornchurch
CF	Chalk Farm	RE*	London Road, Romford
CM*	Chelsham	RG*	Reigate
CN	Carshalton	RL	Rye Lane
CS	Chiswick (non-operational)	S	Shepherds Bush
CT	Clapton	SA*	St.Albans
CY*	Crawley	SJ*	Swanley Junction
D	Dalston	SP	Sidcup
DG*	Dunton Green	ST*	Staines
DS*	Dorking	SV*	Stevenage
DT*	Dartford	SW	Stockwell
E	Enfield	T	Leyton
ED	Elmers End	TB	Bromley
EG*	East Grinstead	TC	Croydon
EP*	Epping	TG*	Tring
EW	Edgware	TH	Thornton Heath
G	Forest Gate	TL	Catford
GD*	Godstone	TW*	Tunbridge Wells
GF*	Guildford	U	Upton Park
GM	Gillingham Street, Victoria	UX	Uxbridge
GR*	Garston	V	Turnham Green
GY*	Grays	W	Cricklewood
H	Hackney	WD	Wandsworth
HD	Harrow Weald	WG	West Green
HE*	High Wycombe	WH	West Ham
HF*	Hatfield	WL	Walworth
HG*	Hertford	WR*	Windsor
HH*	Two Waters	WY*	Addlestone
HW	Southall	X	Middle Row
J	Holloway	-	Aldenham (non-operational)

* indicates a Country Area garage.

The foregoing list represents garages operational at 1st January 1960 plus the two main non-operational sites for bus maintenance.

The changes during the year under review, of which none involved the Country Area were as follows:

Trolleybus Depots becoming Bus Garages:

HB   Hammersmith on 20th July. This did not convert to a bus garage in the normal sense, the new motor bus routes operating from Shepherds Bush instead. It was used however from this date to house the B.E.A. fleet of coaches operated by London Transport, which were moved out of Shepherds Bush.

HL   Hanwell on 9th November.

HT   Highgate on 20th July (still continued to operate trolleybuses as well).

WH   West Ham had already been operating motor buses since 11th November 1959 and was finally completely converted on 27th April).

WW   Walthamstow on 3rd February (still continued to operate trolleybuses as well until 27th April).

Bus Garages Closed:

G   Forest Gate on 27th April. (The bulk of its allocation was transferred to West Ham with a minor number to Upton Park and North Street, Romford. These garages assumed responsibility for the Forest Gate workings).

This particular blind display was added by the compilers in March 1960, which fact conveniently confirms the year during which GS25 is seen departing Onslow Street Bus Station, Guildford. In November it entered works for overhaul and would not re-appear until February of the following year with newly fitted trafficators.
(J.A.S.Hambley collection)

APPENDIX II

Again, a grateful thank you is extended to the following correspondents who have provided helpful comments and information updating or correcting earlier titles in this series of books. Ken Browning, Geoff Burrows, E.G.Cope, John Cummings, P.J.Malsher, Barry Maynard-Smith, George Moon, Geoff W.Morant, Les Stitson and Hugh Taylor.

1939-1945 BOOK

Page 44   S384 was a single deck bus seating 30 passengers and not as stated in the caption.

Page 141   ST998 is in use on the Bents Park Road and Mowbray Road service to Marsden Road. The variation via Westoe Road would have shown Mowbray Road as the destination. A postscript with regard to the conductor can be added in that he served in the First World War receiving an injury to his left arm and hand leaving him limited use of these limbs, although not impairing his ability as a conductor entailing the use of a 'ticket nipper'. Bell Punches were never used on SSCT motor buses.

Page 143   The top picture of ST747 is taken at the Cookbridge Street terminus of the Leeds to Otley and Ilkley services via Lawnswood and Bramhope.

1951 BOOK

Page 129 etc. Several pictures are included in this volume credited to Geoff Morant. No indication was given at the time of the date of the photographs and a check on allocations gave no cause for concern that these were not taken in the latter part of 1951. However, it now transpires that these came from the collection of the late Jack Wyse and an annotation on the folder housing the negatives indicates they may have been taken in 1952.

1959 BOOK

Page 16   The via point blind displayed on RM66 is in fact that for Poplar garage's weekday workings on Route 23.

Page 28   Route 277 replaced trolleybus 677 on 15th April and not the 11th as quoted in the caption to the lower picture which should also be credited to Fred W.Ivey.

Page 48   The RT whose identity is obscured by the cyclist in the lower picture has been identified as RT4771 which entered service during May, having been in store since delivery in August 1954.

Page 29   Needless to say an avid fan of the 'Addicks' has provided the answer to the slightly rhetorical question posed in the bottom caption. For the record the match that day was a fourth round F.A.Cup tie against Everton, the score was 2-2 and 44,094 people attended.

Page 56   It has been pointed out that the number blinds displayed by RT4798 in the top picture and also in the top picture on page 75 appear to be old 179A panels on which the A has been painted out.

Page 68   RT1001 in the upper picture was never resident at Hatfield garage and operates from its normal garage of St. Albans.

Page 80   The further bus in the upper picture is RT3868 which was also overhauled in February 1959.

Page 98   Since the RT on Route 61 in the upper picture is standing driverless in Station Approach at Orpington, it must be assumed that it is in fact turning there on a short working from Eltham as through buses by-passed Station Approach.

Page 120   The Bexley Hospital journeys were in fact taken over on 4th March by an extension of Route 124 which represented a bifurcation from the weekday route which had schoolday journeys to Falconwood Parade via Riefield Road. It was not until 15th May 1960 that the Sunday service including the Bexley Hospital journeys was renumbered 124A.

Page 160   In the Vehicle Index, RT2868 should be shown as appearing on page 55.

VEHICLE INDEX

Class	Number	Page
RT	4490	101
RT	4536	67
RT	4544	78
RT	4582	113
RT	4640	63
RT	4755	104
RT	4772	100
RT	4787	94
RTL	4	121
RTL	4	144
RTL	13	107
RTL	51	32
RTL	52	107
RTL	70	96
RTL	89	38
RTL	96	18
RTL	127	56
RTL	130	91
RTL	173	116
RTL	241	79
RTL	336	107
RTL	440	142
RTL	480	47
RTL	524	45
RTL	641	12
RTL	641	87
RTL	668	132
RTL	741	47
RTL	813	113
RTL	913	149
RTL	931	82
RTL	961	153
RTL	981	150
RTL	1051	150
RTL	1060	26
RTL	1152	86
RTL	1163	48
RTL	1262	106
RTL	1264	89
RTL	1265	110
RTL	1276	77
RTL	1278	40
RTL	1282	89
RTL	1298	74
RTL	1299	100
RTL	1300	105
RTL	1397	42
RTL	1403	107
RTL	1550	47
RTL	1555	105
RTL	1582	85
RTL	1588	70
RTL	1590	25
RTL	1622	37
RTW	6	60
RTW	21	82
RTW	104	108
RTW	130	41
RTW	136	118
RTW	207	154
RTW	215	154
RTW	227	62
RTW	264	121
RTW	278	151
RTW	315	78
RTW	320	108
RTW	472	116
RTW	500	152
RW	2	32
RW	2	115
RW	2	115
SRT	155	140
ST	485	129
ST	513	129
ST	1059	130
STD	74	35
STD	95	128
STL	420	130
STL	537	143
STL	542	139
STL	698	143
STL	868	143
STL	930	143
STL	935	135
STL	1488	138
STL	1511	154
STL	1700	148
STL	1792	143
STL	1889	131
STL	1915	143
STL	2093	43
STL	2093	127
STL	2683	54
STL	2684	145
STL	2685	145
STL	2687	145
STL	2694	104
STL	2695	19
STL	2698	145
T	10	137
T	105	128
T	460	97
T	532	137
T	787	61
T	790	119
T	790	119
T	794	147
Tbus	1336	39
Tbus	1804	143
TD	46	136
TD	84	143
TD	90	53
TF	17	134
TF	29	131
TF	65	133
Service V	447W	66
Service V	650J	127